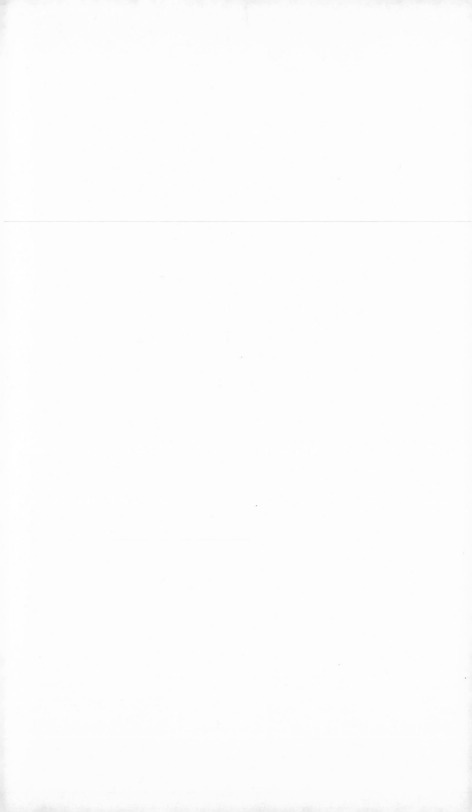

GARLAND STUDIES ON

THE ELDERLY IN AMERICA

edited by

STUART BRUCHEY
UNIVERSITY OF MAINE

A GARLAND SERIES

BURNOUT IN AFRICAN AMERICAN FAMILY CAREGIVERS

NURSING INTERVENTIONS

CATHERINE CASTON

GARLAND PUBLISHING, INC.
NEW YORK & LONDON / 1997

Library of Congress Cataloging-in-Publication Data

Caston, Catherine, 1947–
    Burnout in African American family caregivers : nursing
interventions / Catherine Caston.
        p.   cm. — (Garland studies on the elderly in America)
    Revision of the author's thesis (Ph. D.)—University of Iowa,
1994.
    Includes bibliographical references and index.
    ISBN 0-8153-2647-5 (alk. paper)
    1. Frail elderly—Home care—United States—Psychological
aspects. 2. Afro-American aged—Home care—Psychological
aspects. 3. Caregivers—Job stress—United States. 4. Burn out
(Psychology) 5. Community health services—Utilization—United
States. I. Title. II. Series.
HV1461.C39 1997
362.6—dc21   96-37839

Printed on acid-free, 250-year-life paper
Manufactured in the United States of America

This book is dedicated to all the Primary Family Caregivers and Care Recipients who participated in this study.

Contents

LIST OF TABLES ix

LIST OF FIGURES xiii

I.   INTRODUCTION 3
    Statement of the Problem 5
    Purposes of the Study 5
    Research Hypotheses 5
    Definitions 6
    Assumptions 7
    Significance of the Study 7
    Summary 10

II.   REVIEW OF THE LITERATURE 11
    Self-Esteem 13
    Enmeshment 14
    Caregiver Burden 15
    Caregiver Burnout 16
    Health Services Utilization 16
    Theoretical Framework: Satir Model 18
    Satir Tools 20
    Summary 21

III.   RESEARCH METHODOLOGY 23
    Study Design 23
    Conceptual Model 24
    Selection of the Sample 26
    Instruments 26
    Intervention Protocol 30
    Data Collection and Analysis 48

Human Subjects Approval   48
Pilot Study   48
Summary   49

IV.   ANALYSIS OF DATA   51
Characteristics of the Sample of Care Recipients   51
Results of Care Recipients' Instruments   59
Characteristics of Sample of Primary Family Caregivers   62
Results of Caregivers' Checklist   62
Quantitative Analysis   69
Hypothesis Results   69
Qualitative Analysis   84
Summary of Findings   98

V.   DISCUSSION AND IMPLICATIONS   100
Discussion of Findings   101
Nursing Implications   103
Nursing Practice   104
Nursing Theory and Education   105
Nursing Research   105
Study Limitations   106
Recommendations for Further Study   107
Summary of Findings   108

APPENDIX   111

BIBLIOGRAPHY   123

INDEX   139

List of Tables

1. Demographic Characteristics of the Care Recipient . . . 52

2. Care Recipient's Education Preparation by
    Frequencies and Percent 55

3. Chi-Square Results With Frequencies of Care
    Recipient's Family Relationships by Groups 55

4. Chi-Square Results of Care Recipient's Length
    of Time Being Homebound 56

5. Care Recipient's Reasons for Being Homebound by
    Control and Experimental Group 58

6. Reason for Being Homebound by Length of Time
    Being Homebound (Care Recipient) (N=60) 59

7. Mean Scores for Evaluation of Status of Care
    Recipient Pre- and Post-Intervention by Group 60

8. Mean Differences Between Post- Versus Pre-
    Evaluation Scores 61

9. Care Recipients' Mean Scores Change in Control
    Versus Experimental Groups 61

10. Demographic Characteristics of Primary Family
    Caregiver 64

11. PFC's Level of Education and Usual Occupation 65

12. Frequency Table of Responsibilities Assumed by
     Caregivers 66

13. Frequency Table of Health Service Utilization by
     Control and Experimental Groups Pre- and
     Post-Intervention 67

14. T-Test Differences Between PFCs in Control and
     Experimental Groups at Baseline on Self-Esteem,
     Cohesion, Adaptability, Burden and Burnout 70

15. Cronbach's Alpha Coefficients of PFCs for Study
     Instruments 71

16. Self-Esteem Mean Scores for Evaluation of Primary
     Family Caregivers 72

17. Self-Esteem Mean Differences Between Post- Versus
     Pre-Evaluation of Primary Family Caregivers 73

18. Self-Esteem: T-Test Results of PFCs--Control
     Versus Experimental Groups 73

19. Cohesion and Adaptability Mean Scores and Standard
     Deviations for Evaluation of Status of Primary
     Family Caregivers 74

20. Mean Differences Between Post- Versus Pre-
     Evaluation Cohesion and Adaptation Scores of PFCs . . 75

21. Cohesion and Adaptability T-Test Results of
     Control Versus Experimental Groups 76

22. Chi-Square Analysis of the Care Recipients'
     Dimensions of Religiosity (N=60) 78

23. Chi-Square Analysis of the Dimensions of
     Religiosity of PFCs (N=60) 78

24. Burden and Burnout Mean Scores for Evaluation of
     Primary Family Caregivers 80

25. Burden and Burnout Mean Differences Between Post-
     Versus Pre- Evaluation Scores of PFCs 81

26. Burden and Burnout T-Test Results of Control
     Versus Experimental Groups 82

List of Figures

1. Diagram of Caregiver Burnout Pre- and Post-Intervention 4

2. Experiential Teaching-Learning Cycle 19

3. Conceptual Model 25

4. Mrs. Johnson's Family of Origin Map 43

5. Mrs. Johnson's Maternal Family Map 44

6. Mrs. Johnson's Paternal Family Map 45

7. Mrs. Johnson's Wheel of Influence 46

8. Age Distribution of Care Recipients 54

9. Number of Care Recipients and Years of Family Caregiving (N=60) 57

10. Age Distribution of Primary Family Caregivers 63

11. Diagram of Caregiver Burnout After SDS Intervention . 85

12. The Satir Change Process 86

13. Intervention Protocol: First Level Change Process--Awareness and Acceptance 99

Foreword

With the phenomena of longer life spans and higher medical and long-term care costs, more and more elderly will be taken care of by family members in their homes, rather than in costly care facilities. The emotional costs to family caregivers is well documented in various recent writings. Costs to family caregivers include: (a) frustration, (b) anger, (c) physical and emotional exhaustion, (d) helplessness, (e) depression, and (f) physical health deterioration.

Little effort has been made to focus on helping primary family caregivers besides giving them encouragement and occasional respite, and providing support groups for them.

This book describes the results of a Virginia Satir-based intervention program with African-American primary family caregivers of homebound frail elderly who needed daily assistance with self-care management support.

Dr. Caston developed and tested an intervention program using the world renowned Virginia Satir's family assessment and processing tools. One belief of the Satir model is that people who help others might need assistance in their "helper's role," in order to reduce the stress such work produces and to help them take better care of themselves.

The aim of the program was to help primary family caregivers increase self-esteem, decrease enmeshment with their elderly family members, decrease caregiver burden, decrease potential burnout and increase health services utilization.

Not only does Dr. Caston suggest such possibilities, she actually supports her claims with a highly scientific study. Her study shows that the primary family caregivers increased their self-esteem, decreased their enmeshment with the elderly family member, decreased their caregiver burden and decreased potential burnout. However, her study does not support an increase of health services utilization.

I happen to be very pleased that Dr. Caston's expectation of caregivers increasing health services utilization was not supported by her work. This indicates to me that there was no shift of responsibility from family caregivers to public health services.

I hope this finding will encourage social and health agencies, governments and insurance groups to support this intervention program.

The population studied was African-American primary family caregivers who were looking after persons aged 60 years or older, who were homebound and needed daily assistance.

The results are so positive that one could easily assume that this intervention program for caregivers could be directly applied with all cultural groups of the U.S.A. and other countries.

If the elderly can live longer at home within their family context, their later years could be much happier and more meaningful. Having the elderly cared for by family caregivers often provides opportunities for families to have happier and richer family relationships. It might also give grandchildren more opportunities to enjoy the extended family--something many families have lost by a strong nuclear family orientation in our North American culture.

At times, the primary family caregivers of elderly people are called the "sandwich generation." They are still helping their children grow up, attend school, and start careers while, at the same time, they are called upon to take care of their frail elderly parents. Often the stress is too much for them.

Yet, if they do not help their elderly parents, uncles or aunts, their guilt might take a serious toll on them resulting in anger or depression.

Thus, the value of this intervention program.

Dr. Caston's study and intervention program is timely in terms of helping primary family caregivers and helping families stay closer and more positively connected. The program could also help governments, insurance companies and social/health agencies with opportunities to assist caregivers. Through training program and planned intervention program, communities can be supported to help the elderly live at home with help from caregivers who will not be burned out by doing so.

Dr. John Banmen
Psychologist and Family Therapist
Co-author: *The Satir Model: Family Therapy and Beyond*
The University of British Columbia

Preface

The material presented here is a blending of my psychiatric nursing knowledge, my understanding of the Satir Human Growth Model, and the many African-American family caregivers I have observed in the past 25 years. Familial caregiving can produce a tremendous amount of strain. This strain can lead to burden and burnout.

This book gives supportive evidence that the Satir model can be a nursing intervention with African-American family caregivers. The complete loss of private and professional life among caregivers is all too common in African-American family caregivers. Cultural factors, such as family dynamics and religious commitment, contribute to this loss among African-American caregivers.

The chapters of this book follow the nursing research format and test a nursing intervention model using the Satir family processing tools in order to determine the effectiveness of the model on primary family caregivers (PFCs) who provided 60 to 70 percent of the care of an African-American homebound frail elderly relative without relief for greater than six months.

The blending of nursing and the Satir family model gives supportive evidence that the integration of these conceptual frameworks can be applied in the context of teaching and clinical practice. The strength of the application of this blended model is in the comprehensive clinical procedures which the family health nurse and the family caregiver can develop together in order to decrease burnout.

This book is one of my efforts to decrease burnout among primary family caregivers. Using my experience with family caregivers, I have examined the phenomena of family caregiving and caregiver burnout in an empirical context. I am grateful to my father, Van Caston, my mentor, Virginia Satir, and to Dr. John Banmen, a great teacher and friend. Each gave their blending threads to the completion of this book.

Acknowledgments

I wish to acknowledge those persons who were instrumental in giving me guidance, support and sharing encouraging words throughout my course of study: Curry Miller, Dorothy and Robert Bullock, Lorraine Davis, Priscilla Daniels, Gwendolyn Williams, Kathleen Buckwalter, Dan Russell, Mary Stewart-Dedmon, Meridean Maas, and Toni Tripp-Reimer.

I especially wish to thank Dr. John Banmen of the Satir Avanta Network for his assistance and encouragement throughout this research endeavor.

I particularly want to thank my family and friends; Bill Johnson, my statistician; and, Kathleen Detert for her editorial and typing assistance.

Burnout in African American Family Caregivers

I

Introduction

Self-esteem problems of caregivers have been documented in the literature, but none of the studies linked caregiver burden, caregiver burnout, health services utilization, self-esteem and enmeshment. Similarly, no nursing intervention model provides the primary family caregiver (PFC) with a way to deal with enmeshment, although some nursing interventions have been proposed for caregiver burnout, such as caregiver support groups, respite care, elderly support projects, psychoeducational groups, and social skills training programs (Gallagher-Thompson & Steffen, 1994; Lawton, Brody, & Saperstein, 1991; Miller, Gulle & McCue, 1986; Pinkston & Linsk, 1984; Quayhagen & Quayhagen, 1989; Robinson, 1988; Schaie & Lawton, 1991; Schopler & Galinsky, 1993). However, limitations to these strategies are that the PFC neglects self-fulfilling activities and feels guilty when leaving the care recipient in the care of another person. This scenario may be reflected in the number of studies reporting caregiver reluctance to use health services even though there is a documented need for such care (Skaff & Pearlin, 1992). It was hypothesized that the proposed intervention, Self-Directed Skills Model, by using Satir family assessment and processing tools to decrease enmeshment and caregiver burden and increase health services utilization and self-esteem, would therefore decrease the potential for caregiver burnout (see Figure 1).

Taft (1985) states that self-esteem is a quality of life issue in later life. Nurses can increase social interaction, decrease ageism, and provide an emotional outlet for empowering the elderly's health status. This empowering quality can be enhanced for the frail elderly if the PFC's perception of his or her quality of life is positive and the potential for caregiver burnout is decreased.

3

Predictive Statement Before SDS is Applied to Caregiver

Low Self-Esteem + Low Service Utilization +
High Caregiver Burden + High Enmeshment =
High Caregiver Burnout

Hypothesized Results After SDS Has Been Applied

High Self-Esteem + Low Enmeshment +
Low Caregiver Burden + High Service Utilization =
Decreased Caregiver Burnout

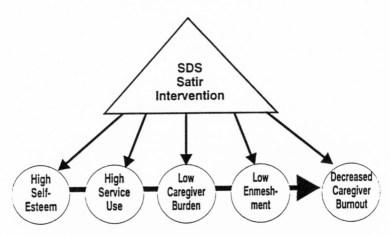

Figure 1. Diagram of Caregiver Burnout Pre- and Post-Intervention

PFCs take on the responsibility of providing extensive care to frail homebound elderly. This study was designed to test the effects of long-term caregiving on PFCs. This chapter serves as an introduction to the research and indicates the statement of the problem, research questions, purposes of the study, and research hypotheses. In addition, the operational definitions, assumptions, and limitations of the study are also presented.

STATEMENT OF THE PROBLEM

The primary aim of this study was to evaluate the effectiveness of a Self-Directed Skills (SDS) Nursing Intervention Model on increasing self-esteem and service utilization and decreasing enmeshment, burden and burnout in African-American primary family caregivers. The overall research question tested was: What is the effect of the SDS intervention on self-esteem, service utilization, enmeshment, burden and burnout in African-American family caregivers of homebound frail elderly?

PURPOSES OF THE STUDY

The purposes of this research were to test a nursing intervention, Self-Directed Skills (SDS), by determining the effectiveness of the intervention on the PFC who provides 60 to 75 percent of the care for an African-American homebound frail elderly relative. The study specifically aimed to: (1) implement and evaluate the SDS nursing intervention model using the Satir paradigm, and (2) evaluate the differences between the experimental and control groups on levels of self-esteem, enmeshment, service utilization, burden and burnout.

RESEARCH HYPOTHESES

The following research hypotheses were tested:

1. Subjects in the experimental group will report a higher level of self-esteem after administration of the SDS intervention compared to subjects in the control group.

2. There will be a decreased level of enmeshment following the SDS intervention for the experimental subjects compared to subjects in the control group.
3. There will be increased use of health services utilization among experimental subjects compared to subjects in the control group following SDS intervention.
4. There will be decreased caregiver burden and caregiver burnout in experimental subjects after SDS intervention compared to subjects in the control group.

DEFINITIONS

The following definitions were used for the study:

Primary Family Caregiver: One who cares for a frail, dependent African-American elderly relative in the home 60 to 75 percent of the day, without relief, for greater than six months. The caregiver met the following criteria: was a relative, lived within a 100-mile radius of the Greater New Orleans area, spoke English, and was able to read and write. The criteria for inclusion were assessed during the initial interview using the Care Recipient Demographic Data Sheet.

Self-Directed Skills: This intervention model was an adaptation of Virginia Satir's Family Assessment and Processing Tools (see Appendix). The Satir paradigm has as its core concept, the self ("I am") through which the process of change evolves. Self-esteem and enmeshment are viewed as internal resources through which an individual lives his life (Satir, et al., 1991). The PFCs of frail homebound elderly can be classified as caregivers in which change is predicated on internal resources. How do the PFCs cope (making that internal shift) in carrying out their caregiving tasks? The SDS intervention model was the goal of the Satir paradigm in this research study. SDS externalized the PFC's internal way of coping. The self is validated through the researcher focusing on the PFC's relationship, his view of himself/herself, the context (caregiving), and how the PFC views the change process.

Chronically Ill Frail Elderly: African-American persons, aged 60 and older, who were homebound and needed assistance in at least two ADLs as measured by Katz' Activity of Daily Living (ADL) Index and/or who had dementia according to the Kahn Mental Status Questionnaire (MSQ) and were in need of assistance with self-care management skills from a family member.

Enmeshment: Emotional closeness in family relations where family members maintain the status quo and submerge issues of conflict. The investigator used the Family Adaptability and Cohesions Evaluation Scales II (FACES II) to measure cohesion (Olson, et al., 1991). Higher scores on cohesion indicate very connected rather than enmeshed. High scores on adaptability are best described as very flexible rather than chaotic. The Clinical Rating Scale (CRS) was used to measure the researcher's observational assessment of the PFCs. The CRS assumed that there is a curvilinear relationship between cohesion and adaptability of family members. Olson stated that separated and connected scores indicate moderate cohesion. A balance between too little closeness is called disengaged and too much closeness is enmeshment in the family. Adaptability was represented by moderate scores, meaning a structured and flexible family. Too little adaptability was viewed as rigid and too much adaptability indicated chaotic (Thomas & Olson, 1993).

Self-Esteem: A behavioral concept that allows the person to value himself/herself and to treat oneself with dignity, love and reality. Rosenberg's Self-Esteem Scale was used to measure the self-esteem of the primary family caregiver (Rosenberg, 1965). Higher scores indicate high self-esteem.

Caregiver Burden: Loss of hope and feeling overwhelmed by care responsibilities and daily hassles. The Zarit Caregiver Burden Inventory was used to measure this concept (Zarit, 1985). Higher scores indicate greater caregiver burden.

Caregiver Burnout: Responding to overload of caregiving tasks. To accommodate family caregivers' wording, a revised version of the Maslach Burnout Inventory was used to measure caregiver burnout (Maslach & Jackson, 1986). Higher scores indicate increased caregiver burnout.

Health Services Utilization: Any type of formal assistance given to the family caregiver of a frail homebound relative. These data were collected during the initial interview using the form "Use of Care Program."

ASSUMPTIONS

Assumptions of the Satir model underlying this study were:

1. People are unique.
2. Change is possible. Even if external change is limited, internal change is possible.
3. We all have the internal resources we need in order to cope successfully and to grow.
4. Most people choose familiarity over comfort, especially during times of stress.
5. People learn survival/coping in their family of origin.
6. People are basically good. They need to find their own "treasure" to connect and validate their own self-worth.
7. Appreciating and accepting the past increases our ability to manage our present. The past does not have to contaminate the present.
8. Congruence and high self-esteem are major goals in the SDS nursing intervention model.
9. All behavior is purposeful.
10. Healthy human relationships are built on equality of values (Satir, et al., 1991).

The researcher is a member of the Satir Avanta Network and has taken 12 semester hours of formal coursework in the Satir process-oriented model.

SIGNIFICANCE OF THE STUDY

This research examined the home care of frail elderly African-Americans who were cared for by PFCs. Specifically, the effects of the SDS intervention (Satir tools) on self-esteem, health services utilization, enmeshment, burden and burnout on African-America family caregivers of homebound frail elderly were studied. An experimental pre- and post-control research design was used with 60 African-American PFCs

(30 in each group). The intervention was aimed at increasing self-esteem and health services utilization and decreasing enmeshment, burden and burnout in PFCs of elderly homebound care recipients.

This study contributes to the present body of knowledge in aging and African-American family caregivers. There has been no research suggesting a relationship between self-esteem, enmeshment, burden, burnout and health services utilization and the use of the Satir family tools with African-American PFCs and elderly care recipients. Therefore, if high self-esteem of the PFCs who care for frail elderly African-Americans in the home can enhance the caring process, decrease caregiver burden, caregiver burnout and enmeshment, and increase health services utilization, both the caregiver and care recipient will benefit.

By using the Satir family tools as a nursing intervention model, nurses can affect family health nursing interventions in the community and provide a foundation for health care policy/ legislative outcomes for the elderly who are frail and homebound. PFCs using the Satir family tools may foster the practice of gerontological, family and community health nursing, thus promoting a healthier lifestyle for the PFC and contributing to an improved quality of life for the elderly homebound care recipient.

Use of the Satir family tools by PFCs in home health care of frail elderly care recipients may make a difference in the PFC's effectiveness in dealing with caregiving responsibilities. In this study, the comparison of the effects of the SDS intervention (Satir family tools) on the experimental group versus friendly visits with the control group may add significant information regarding home health care of frail African-American elderly.

The nurse-client relationship has always been a challenge to the gerontological nurse. The essence of the relationship is to facilitate the individual's knowledge of himself/herself. This knowledge provides the foundation for self-awareness, self-management, and self-acceptance.

The emotional cost of caregiving is well documented in the literature (Archer & MacLean, 1993; Babins, Killion & Merovitz, 1988; Baillie, Norbeck & Barnes, 1988; Beekman, 1991; Biegel, Sales & Schulz, 1991; Bliesner & Alley, 1990; Brody, 1986; Chenoweth & Spencer, 1986; George & Gwyther, 1986; Gerstel & Gallagher, 1993; Kahana, Biegel & Wykle, 1994; McFall & Miller, 1992; Montgomery, Gonyea & Hooyman, 1985; Moritz, Kasl & Ostfeld, 1992; Morris, Morris & Britton, 1988; Morycz, 1985; Motenko, 1989; Pilisik & Parks, 1988;

Roybal, 1987; Stone, Cafferata & Sange, 1987; Townsend, 1990; Zarit, Reever & Bach-Peterson, 1980; Zarit, Orr & Zarit, 1985). Problems cited in the literature that are reflective of caregiver burden that lead to caregiver burnout are: caregiver role strain; physical health deterioration; clinical depression; constriction of social life; feelings of guilt and resentment; frustration, anger, helplessness and grief; and physical and emotional exhaustion. The SDS intervention tested in this study could potentially decrease emotional cost of the PFC.

SUMMARY

The purpose of this research was to test a nursing intervention model for African-American primary family caregivers of frail homebound elderly in the home. Satir's paradigm was the conceptual model used because it facilitates study of self-esteem, the family de-enmeshment process, caregiver burden and burnout, and the use of health service agencies.

The design of the study was a pre-test, post-test experimental design. This research provided information on PFC self-esteem, enmeshment, burden, burnout, and health services utilization for the frail homebound elderly before and after a nursing intervention based on the Satir model. Other potential benefits of this study were to facilitate care recipient quality of care by increasing use of formal and informal health services, thus allowing caregivers to continue in their roles without endangering their health and well-being.

II

Literature Review

Review of the literature on filial responsibility and African-American family caregivers as a population in need of an intervention for self-management skills. Research on the effects of caregiving on PFCs of African-Americans is reviewed within the context of the Satir family processing tools.

The SDS nursing intervention model is presented as a therapeutic intervention which enhances the self-growth of the PFC (Satir, et al., 1991). The two main concepts of the Satir model are self-esteem and enmeshment. Caregiver burden, caregiver burnout and health services utilization are the variables that will be affected if the self-esteem and enmeshment of the PFC are improved in a positive manner. This presumed benefit of the SDS intervention model will be developed from the review of the literature on self-esteem, enmeshment, health services utilization, caregiver burden, caregiver burnout and the Satir paradigm.

The United States Census Bureau reports that the total population for African-Americans in the United States in 1994 was 33 million. The percent distribution of African-Americans who were 65 years of age and over was 8.2 percent (Bennett, 1995). Brody (1986) and Pilisik and Parks (1988) stated that 80 percent of homebound elderly receive care from family members over longer periods of time than ever before. Filial responsibility in health care will continue to escalate and caring for chronically ill older African-American persons will continue to be a major concern in the United States (Hines-Martin, 1992; Schulz & O'Brien, 1994; Townsend, 1990; Zarit & Whitlatch, 1992). Although the number of African-American family caregivers is not documented in the literature, African-American health status continues to lag behind whites (Fredman, Doly & Lazur, 1995; Maddox, 1987; U.S. Congress Select Committee on Aging--House of Representatives, 1988; Wykle,

1994) and deserves further attention from gerontological nurse researchers.

Chatters, Taylor and Jackson (1985) noted that extended family members become support networks for elderly African-Americans. They studied 581 respondents who were over 55 years of age. Their results supported previous findings that availability and family factors influence informal networking support in caring for elderly African-Americans.

Morycz, Malloy, Bozich and Martz (1987) examined data from 810 patients in a community-based geriatric assessment center, noting racial differences in the family burden of caregiving. The results, when controlled for race, showed that there were no essential differences among the races (22% of the black population and about 25% of the white population) in the experience of family burden as a social problem.

Taylor (1985) studied 581 African-Americans aged 55 and older to examine the extent to which informal support is provided by extended family members. The results showed a significant level of kinship interaction patterns, and support networks were present in the family of the elderly African-American. Hines-Martin (1992) reviewed the literature in regard to the family caregivers of chronically ill African-American elderly and found that African-American caregivers play a unique role in providing home care for their frail elderly relative. Both Taylor and Hines-Martin provide evidence that African-American caregiving is a family involvement process.

Since the 1960s, there has been a growing trend in elderly caregiver research to include more minority subjects. Morycz, Malloy, Bozich and Martz's (1987) study showed some variability in the status of the African-American caregivers as compared to the status of white caregivers. However, nursing research on aging among the African-American population remains largely underdeveloped (Johnson & Barner, 1990). Therefore, this study, which measures the self-esteem, enmeshment, burden, burnout, and service utilization before and after a nursing intervention (SDS model) of African-American family caregivers, makes a unique contribution to the nursing knowledge base and literature. The SDS model is designed to impact the caregiver's self-esteem, enmeshment, burden, burnout, and service utilization (see Figure 1). These concepts are reviewed in detail below.

SELF-ESTEEM

The relationship of self-esteem to the primary family caregiver is dependent upon how the individual's psychological make-up interacts with his/her self-percepts and his/her view of power and control (Satir, Banmen, Gerber & Gomori, 1991). Stanwyck (1983) noted that a person's self-esteem cannot survive when unnourished by others. Caregiver morbidity studies have indicated that family caregiving causes caregiver burden, emotional exhaustion, displaced anger, caregiver burnout, stress, role strain, depression with low morale, and low self-esteem (Archbold, Stewart, Greenlick & Harvath, 1990; Bowers, 1990; Bull, 1990; Cafferata, 1989; Chenoweth & Spencer, 1986; Cohen & Eisdorfer, 1988; Dellasega, 1991; Lindgren, 1990; Morris, Morris & Britton, 1988; Neary, 1993; Ogus, 1990; O'Neill, 1991; Pruchno & Potashnik, 1989; Sime, 1990).

Muhlenkam and Sayles (1986) studied 98 adults to identify the relationships among perceived social support, self-esteem and positive health practices. The results showed that self-esteem and social support are positive indicators for life-style health management. Family caregivers can be viewed as individuals whose self-esteem is influenced by the need for open communication and family support. Yet studies on caregiver morbidity have indicated that caregivers are at risk for decreased psychological well-being.

Thomas (1988) examined the self-esteem and life satisfaction of 21 elderly African-American females in relation to which treatment practice, meditation/relaxation or didactic stress management, resulted in greater self-esteem and life satisfaction. Neugarten, Havighurst and Tobin's (1961) Life Satisfaction Indices A and B, Rosenberg's (1965) Self-Esteem Scale, and a self-report of health problems and activities were used to assess the variables under study. Findings suggested that life satisfaction and self-esteem were significantly improved for African-American elderly women who participated in the meditation/relaxation training group, a self-directed method.

There are no well documented studies that measure self-esteem in family caregivers and none related to self-esteem of African-American caregivers. Therefore, it is important to understand the influence continuous caregiving has on the African-American caregiver's self-esteem.

ENMESHMENT

With regard to caring for elderly parents, Satir (1961) views enmeshment as "burdened with responsibility of living for the parents. The person's own needs are ignored and he has never discovered a way of getting them met. As a result he swings from omnipotence to helplessness from grandiosity to decreased self-worth" (p. 61). Caregivers repeat the familiar patterns they learned while growing up, even if the patterns are dysfunctional. Their perception of the care recipient is that they are responsible for them (Satir & Banmen, 1983; Satir, Banmen, Gerber & Gomori, 1991).

Wood (1985) studied interconnectedness among families who went to the Philadelphia Child Guidance Clinic for therapy, and analyzed two component concepts: proximity (interpersonal boundaries) and generational hierarchy (subsystem boundaries). The results suggested that proximity and hierarchy are reliable, valid and independent measures of family interconnectedness. The hypothesis that families with high enmeshment are characterized by high degrees of proximity in conjunction with weak hierarchy was not supported. Findings showed that families with strong hierarchy were also enmeshed.

Olson, Sprenkle and Russell (1979) developed and tested a model of family behaviors. They postulated that a balance between cohesion and adaptability within the family system was most functional to the marital and family system. Enmeshed systems were viewed as having too much closeness, while systems with too little closeness were viewed as disengaged. Change in the family system was seen in the context of adaptation. A family adapting to too much change was seen as chaotic, whereas too little adaptation to change led to rigidity in the family system.

Caregivers of frail homebound African-American elderly are likely to have an enmeshment-type relationship because of their sense of commitment and obligation. The African-American caregiver continually accommodates the care recipient and denies his/her own well-being (Jackson, 1970; Jaynes & Williams, 1989; Mutran, 1985; Taylor & Chatters, 1991). This process of denial may lead to low self-esteem, high enmeshment, high caregiver burden, and low use of health services such as respite care, adult day care and nurse aides, thus resulting in caregiver burnout (see Figure 1).

CAREGIVER BURDEN

Home care of the frail elderly affects the family system. Many researchers have identified the family caregiver's role as one of burden (Alley, 1988; Ballie, Norbeck & Barnes, 1988; Bowers, 1990; Bull, 1990; Francell, Conn & Gray, 1988; Harrison & Cole, 1991; Hogan, 1990; Montgomery, Gonyear & Hooyman, 1985; Vitaliano, Young & Russo, 1991; Wykle & Segan, 1991; Zarit, Reever & Bach-Peterson, 1980). Montgomery, et al. (1985) characterized caregiving burden as either subjective or objective. Eighty caregivers participated in the Montgomery study and different factors were found to be related to different types of burden. For example, the best predictors of subjective burden were age and income. In contrast, caregiving tasks that confined the caregiver geographically best predicted objective burden. The researchers suggested increasing the self-care activities of the care recipient and using support devices, respite care and nurse aide services as interventions to relieve the caregiver's objective burden. No interventions were suggested for the relief of subjective burden.

Zarit, Reever and Bach-Peterson (1980) studied family caregivers of elderly persons with senile dementia and identified only one source of caregiver burden: the frequency of family members' visits. These investigators suggested that family caregivers receive increased informal social support from family members in order to ease excessive feelings of burden.

Ballie, Norbeck and Barnes (1988) investigated the stress level of 87 caregivers who maintained their frail elderly family member in the community. Results suggested that social support among caregivers is essential to stress reduction for the caregiver. The researchers suggested that professionals develop strategies to assist and give emotional support to the caregiver, as was done in this study. Wykle and Segal (1991) noted that most African-American caregivers use religion, prayer and faith to decrease caregiver stress and burden but white caregivers use formal health care agencies. Investigators have noted that white caregivers have a higher incidence of burden than African-American caregivers (Hinrichsen & Ramirez, 1992; Marycz, Malloy, Bozich & Martz, 1987; Mui, 1992).

CAREGIVER BURNOUT

Burnout is defined as a "state in which individuals expect little reward and considerable punishment from work" (Meier, 1983, p. 899). Burnout among family caregivers is related to their physical and mental state. It is a gradual process that occurs as a result of stressful events that extend over periods of time during the caregiving relationship (Crossman, London & Barry, 1981; Goldstein, 1979; Maslach & Jackson, 1981).

African-American PFCs need to be evaluated to determine if burnout occurs in their lives as a result of their unrelenting caregiving responsibilities. Burnout results from unrewarding relationships, jobs, and way of life (Ansell, 1981; Patrick, 1979). Maslach and Jackson (1981) noted that burnout is emotional strain that can be measured as emotional exhaustion, depersonalization and lack of personal accomplishment. Burnout decreased the personal relationship between the PFC and the recipient of care (Ogus, 1990).

Family caregiver burnout can be considered to be individualistic and progressive (Jacobson, 1983; Lindgren, 1990; McElroy, 1982; Sime, 1990). As caregiving responsibilities increase, depersonalization of the care recipient may occur. The caregiver may show signs and symptoms of burnout, such as expressed sense of failure, isolation and withdrawal, feeling tired and exhausted all day, a feeling of being immobilized, sleep and gastrointestinal disturbance, frequent headaches and use of tranquilizers (Jacobson, 1983; McElroy, 1982; Patrick, 1979).

Family caregiver burnout research in nursing is limited, yet the emotional component of the burden of professional caregivers has been documented as feelings of unrelenting despair, frustration and meaninglessness (Crossman, London & Barry, 1981; Goldstein, 1979; Ogus, 1990), thus giving the researcher a framework to assess primary family caregiver burnout as a result of low self-esteem and increased enmeshment and burden.

HEALTH SERVICES UTILIZATION

African-Americans continue to have a higher incidence of chronic illnesses than other ethnic groups (Heyman, Fillenbaum, Prosnitz, Raiford, Burchett & Clark, 1991; Hines-Martin, 1992; Kart, 1991; Roybal, 1987; U.S. Congress Select Committee on Aging--House of

Representatives, 1988). Petchers and Milligan (1988) suggested that health services for the black elderly (an underserved population) must be improved through health policy development. Health services utilization of the African-American elderly is dependent upon the individual's ability to pay for the cost of care (Roybal, 1987; U.S. Congress Select Committee on Aging--House of Representatives, 1988). For example, Wykle and Segal (1991) stated that African-American caregivers use religion as a means of coping with caregiving responsibilities, while their white cohorts ask for help from professionals and use problem-solving methods in caregiving situations. Krause (1992) studied the effect of religion on the stress levels of elderly blacks and found that, after controlling for informal emotional support, religion promoted their psychological well-being. Thus there is evidence that religion is an important coping resource for elderly blacks and their PFCs.

Caregivers' use of formal health services for assistance was examined by Smerglia, Deimling and Barresi (1988); their results showed that African-Americans had a greater number of kin available than whites. Roybal (1987) reported that utilization of health services by African-American caregivers occurs only when the caregiver cannot meet the care recipient's needs. Kart (1991) studied the variation in long-term care services of aged African-Americans (55 and over) and found that of the 1,217 respondents, only 11.9% reported using a senior center.

Several types of service utilization interventions are noted in the literature. They include social support, group therapy, self-help groups, adult day care, respite care centers, rest homes, formalized institutionalizational care, friend/kinship networks, case management, community home health care and self-management skills programs (Hernandez, 1991; Hinrichsen & Ramirez, 1992; Hooyman & Lustbader, 1986; Horne, 1985; Kinney, 1979; Levin, 1989; Neary, 1993; Nolan & Grant, 1992; Seltzer, Litchfield, Kapust & Mayer, 1992; Shanas, 1979).

Despite this variety of service intervention strategies that African-American family caregivers might use in providing relief from their caregiving tasks, elderly African-Americans tend to restrict their support networks to children, spouses, neighbors and friends (Billingsley, 1970; Cantor, 1979; Chatter, Taylor & Jackson, 1985; Chatter, Taylor & Jackson, 1986; Mindel, Wright & Starrett, 1986; Sheehan, Wilson & Marella, 1988; Taylor & Chatter, 1991).

In summary, African-American family caregivers use formal services selectively for physical and psychological support. Their use of informal networks seems to outweigh their use of formal health care services. The SDS nursing intervention model used in this research facilitated an experiential self-management strategy for African-American family caregivers. These self-management skills are hypothesized to decrease levels of enmeshment, burden, and burnout and, therefore, to increase levels of self-esteem and service utilization.

THEORETICAL FRAMEWORK: SATIR MODEL

Using the Satir model, the researcher in this study explored caregiver burden as defined by Banmen (1991) as loss of hope and feeling overwhelmed and caregiver burnout, defined as response to overload (Banmen, 1991). The Satir model provided the researcher with a framework for using the Self-Directed Skills (SDS) intervention.

The Experiential Teaching-Learning Cycle (ETLC) was designed by the researcher as a processing tool for the SDS protocol (see Figure 2). The ETLC has the self, context and other as its central focus points and is characterized by four components: (1) making contact, (2) connecting, (3) observing, and (4) processing. Each component overlaps and forms a continuous interactive relationship with the others that is not static.

Making contact was the first segment of the ETLC. It demonstrated how the researcher developed rapport and trust with the PFC. Segment two was called connecting. This segment demonstrated how the investigator tapped the internal resources of the PFC and bridged the verbal and nonverbal content of the PFC with the present context and the care recipient. Observing was the third component of the ETLC. The researcher tracked, wove and reframed the interaction of the PFC, thus adding to the PFC's internal resources in order to promote second-level change. Satir and her colleagues termed this second-level change "transformation" (Satir, Banmen, Gerber & Gomori, 1991). The last segment of the ETLC was called processing. In processing, the researcher continued to tap the PFC's internal resources and processed the content into new learnings. Satir termed this process anchoring the new learnings so as to facilitate self-awareness and personal growth (Satir, Banmen, Gerber & Gomori, 1991).

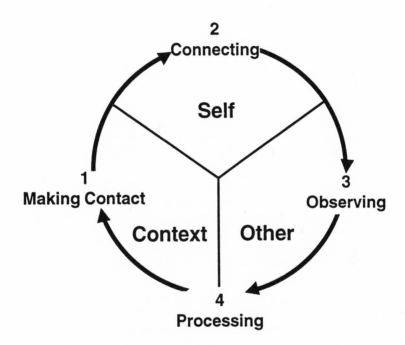

Figure 2. Experiential Teaching-Learning Cycle

The ETLC was a creative process that added new behaviors rather than getting rid of old behaviors. Some basic assumptions underlying the Satir model were: (1) change is possible; (2) therapy focuses on health and possibilities instead of pathology; (3) the individual is his own choice maker; (4) the problem is not the problem: coping is the problem; (5) the therapist and the individual cannot change past events, only the effects they represent; (6) the higher the individual's self-worth, the more wholesome is the coping; (7) process is the avenue of change; (8) content forms the context in which change takes place; and, (9) change takes place at various levels (Satir, Banmen, Gerber & Gomori, 1991).

SATIR TOOLS

Satir used a resource basket of tools as therapeutic interventions for building a systematic approach for viewing family dynamics. She believed that learnings of the individual come from the primary triad--mother, father and the child. The family tools are making contact, family map of origin, the paternal and maternal family maps, communication stances, wheel of influence, the iceberg, map reading, change process, metaphors, sculpting and processing of new behaviors (learnings) (see Satir, et al., 1991, for a complete delineation of the tools).

According to Satir, the researcher would complete the family of origin and paternal and maternal maps of the caregiver. The caregiver would also share his family rules. The researcher would tap the internal resources of the caregiver (his feelings, yearnings and unfinished business), noting patterns and tracking, weaving and reframing the interaction as necessary. Throughout the encounter, the researcher is connecting and reconnecting with the caregiver so as to build on the surfaced data. This helps the caregiver resolve present problems, yearnings, expectations, perceptions, and feelings. The caregiver verbalizes his communication stance and coping and stress patterns. This process will capture and anchor the caregiver's learnings, noting congruent communication, self-care behaviors, and self-esteem messages.

The caregiver yearns for completeness, but past events cause him to react incongruently in the present, thus causing him to have a low self-esteem, increased enmeshment, increased caregiver burden and burnout, and low use of health care agencies. To facilitate high self-esteem, decreased enmeshment, decreased burden and burnout, and increased use of health service agencies, the nurse-therapist surfaces the incongruent information and provides the caregiver with an experience in the present, thus causing a transformation process to take place. This transformation process illuminates the present context and provides a healthier learning experience. The learning experience provides the caregiver with a positive encounter which develops his/her internal resources and produces responsible self-management patterns (Satir & Baldwin, 1983).

SUMMARY

A review of the literature suggested there was no preferred intervention model to reduce family caregiver burnout; however, the literature implied that caregiver role strain, physical health deterioration, clinical depression, constriction of social life, feelings of guilt and resentment, physical and emotional exhaustion, and stress are precursors to caregiver burnout. It has been well documented that caregiver burden arises from performing or assisting in activities of daily living, cognitive incapacity and disruptive behavior of the care recipient, and lack of sociability of the frail homebound elderly (Aneshensel, Pearlin, Mullan, Zarit & Whitlatch, 1995; Chenoweth & Spencer, 1986; Cohen & Eisdorfer, 1988; Motenko, 1989; Poulshock & Deimling, 1984; Townsend, 1990; Zarit & Whitlatch, 1992). Factors known to increase burnout may also diminish self-esteem and increase enmeshment. Thus, caregiver burden and burnout can be viewed as problems that are amenable to nursing interventions that promote self-esteem and diminish enmeshment.

African-American elderly health care research has increased over the past decade (Gibson, 1989; Hernandez, 1991; Lawton, Rajagopal, Brody & Kleban, 1992), but there is a need for nursing intervention studies of African-Americans who provide home care for the frail elderly. The Satir model was the focus of the present study and the Self-Directed Skills (SDS) was the intervention tested. The SDS model uses self-esteem and enmeshment as the two key variables to promote PFCs' self-worth and self-management. The Satir paradigm has, as its cornerstone to therapy and education, the Satir change process. Since change is possible, the researcher developed the SDS nursing intervention model to facilitate this change. Therefore, the Satir paradigm was the driving model for this literature review.

III

Research Methodology

This chapter describes the research design and methods utilized in the study. The researcher tested the differences between 30 experimental group and 30 control group primary family caregivers of frail elderly homebound African-Americans with regard to self-esteem, caregiver burden and burnout, enmeshment and health services utilization. Subjects were contacted through local African-American churches within a 100-mile radius of New Orleans, Louisiana. Each care recipient was assessed using the Katz Activity of Daily Living Index and the Kahn Mental Status Questionnaire. The primary family caregiver (PFC) completed Zarit's Burden Inventory, Maslach's Burnout Inventory, Rosenberg's Self-Esteem Scale, Olson's Family Adaptability Cohesions Evaluation Scale (FACES II), and the Clinical Rating Scale. Findings were analyzed using paired t-test, chi-square, and descriptive statistics.

STUDY DESIGN

The study design was experimental. This methodology provided a framework for testing hypotheses by manipulating and controlling variables under study and randomly assigning research participants to treatment and control conditions. The key dependent variables for this study were self-esteem, enmeshment, caregiver burden, burnout, and service utilization. Extraneous variables included marital status, social position, financial resources, age and sex of caregiver and family support. Potentially intervening variables, which flow from the Satir model, were communication, influence, position in the family and how the caregivers viewed change. An attempt was made to control extraneous and intervening variables by random assignment of the sample participants. To assess comparability of the experimental and control groups at baseline, data were collected on subjects in both groups by the researcher during a two-hour initial interview.

CONCEPTUAL MODEL

The conceptual model used in this research outlines the predetermined, determined and reciprocal effects of family caregiver burnout in caring for the frail homebound elderly. This model is illustrated in Figure 3.

The empirical component shows correlational relationships between the caregiver and care recipient. The care recipient component has a directional relationship with the person's activities of daily living (ADL) and his/her mental status. This directional relationship interacts with the care responsibilities of the caregiving, forming a reciprocal relationship that manifests into self-esteem, enmeshment, caregiving burden and caregiver burnout issues.

The operational component of the conceptual framework shows the instruments that measured the identified dependent variables of the study. These instruments (described in a following section) have established validity and reliability. The demographic profile captured the relationship of the care recipient and caregiver, and the care responsibilities of the latter.

The ADL and mental status of the care recipient were measured by the Katz ADL Index (Katz, et al., 1963) and the Mental Status Questionnaire by Kahn (1960). Several other tools were also used. Rosenberg's Self-Esteem Inventory (Rosenberg, 1965) was used to assess caregiver self-esteem; the Family Adaptability Cohesions Evaluation Scale (FACES II) and the Clinical Rating Scale (Olson, et al., 1985) measured enmeshment; the Zarit Caregiver Burden Inventory (Zarit, et al., 1985) was used to measure caregiver burden; and caregiver burnout was measured by an adaptation of the Maslach Burnout Inventory (Maslach & Jackson, 1986). Finally, the self-directed skills (SDS) nursing intervention tool was used with the experimental group to intervene in the caregiver/care recipient interactional relationship. Friendly home visits of equal duration were used with control group research participants (see procedure for control group in this chapter).

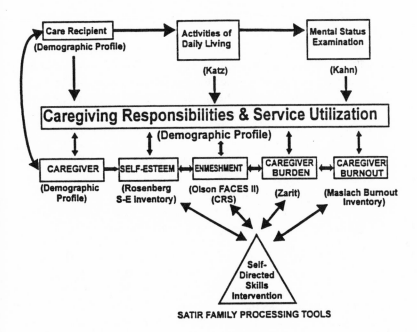

Figure 3. Conceptual Model

SELECTION OF THE SAMPLE

The population for both the pilot and major studies were African-American primary family caregivers of homebound frail elderly persons who provided 60 to 75 percent of daily care for greater than six months without relief. The sample for both the experimental and control groups was selected from local African-American community churches within a 100-mile radius of New Orleans. Public service announcements were also aired on local African-American radio stations and published in church bulletins and in the newspaper. The sample consisted of nine primary family caregivers for the pilot study and 60 for the definitive study.

As noted earlier, the researcher attempted to control extraneous variables by random assignment of subjects to groups. A table of random numbers was used to assign the research participants after initial contact with the researcher had been established and informed consent had been obtained. Replacement of research participants who dropped out was accomplished by using the same procedure outlined above.

INSTRUMENTS

The following tools were used to measure the key concepts in this study. The researcher obtained permission to use all copyrighted instruments from the appropriate sources.

Self-Esteem

Self-esteem was measured by scores on the Rosenberg Self-Esteem Scale (RSE) (Rosenberg, 1965). Using the Guttman Scale version of RSE, self-esteem scores were divided into high, medium and low. Rosenberg (1965) studied 5,024 students from a random selection of ten New York State high school students using the RSE. The Guttman Scale yielded scores from 0 to 6, with a mean of 1.89, standard deviation of 1.44 and skewness of 0.648. High self-esteem equals 0 and 1 (44.8% of subjects), medium self-esteem equals 2 (25.1% of subjects) and low self-esteem equals 3 to 6 (30.0% of subjects). Internal consistency reliability for the New York State sample showed a Cronbach's alpha of 0.77. Test-retest reliability for the RSE was established during a two-week interval by Silber and Tippett in 1965, who studied 28 college students using the RSE and obtained a correlation coefficient of 0.85. Byrne (1983) retested 990 urban Canadian high school students during a seven-month interval and obtained a correlation coefficient of 0.63 (Wylie, 1989).

Enmeshment

Enmeshment was measured by scores on the Family Adaptability and Cohesions Evaluation Scales II (FACES II), as designed by Olson, Portner and Bell (1981). FACES II is a 30-item scale that yields scores in cohesion and adaptability from low to high. Olson, Portner and Bell related the dimensions (cohesion and adaptability) as concepts that measure the degree to which the family system is flexible and able to change, thus relating family structure, role relationships and rules in response to situational and developmental stress. Cohesion and adaptability measure the levels of disengagement and enmeshment in the Family Adaptability and Cohesions Evaluation Scales. In FACES II, the alpha reliability for cohesion was 0.95 and 0.94 for adaptability (Olson, Portner and Bell, 1981).

In 1991, Olson administered FACES II to 2,412 subjects in a national survey of "normal" families. Internal consistency reliability was established using Cronbach's Alpha for each scale (cohesion and adaptability). Scores were computed for each split sample and for the total sample with cohesion ($r=0.87$), adaptability ($r=0.78$) and a total scale ($r=0.90$). Therefore, the internal consistency reliability was adequate for both cohesion and adaptability and the reliability was replicated across the sample (Olson, 1991).

The Clinical Rating Scale (CRS) contains specific indicators and was used to operationally measure cohesion, adaptability and communication of the family being studied. There were four levels of family cohesion, ranging from extremely low cohesion (disengaged) to extremely high cohesion (enmeshed). Separated and connected have been labeled moderate or balanced levels of family functioning. Family adaptability (change) ranged from extremely low adapatability (rigid) to extremely high adaptability (chaotic). Flexible and structured are labeled moderate or balanced levels.

Three levels of communication were also assessed as high, medium and low. A global rating scale indicated the results of the overall evaluation or gestalt rather than a sum of of the sub-scale ratings.

Internal consistency (alpha) of the CRS was 0.95 for cohesion, 0.94 for adaptability, and 0.97 for communication.

Thomas and Olson (1993) advocated using FACES II (self-report) and the CRS so as to obtain a more comprehensive evaluation of the family functions (Fitterer, 1994). Olson and Killorin (1985) developed the CRS for clinicians and researchers to observe and classify family functions based on the clinical interview and/or structured experiences.

Caregiver Burden

Caregiver burden was measured by scores on the Burden Interview (Zarit, Orr & Zarit, 1985). This 22-item inventory evaluates the subjective impact of caregiving using a Likert-type scale with a 0 to 4 response for each item. A total burden score from 0 to 88 is calculated to indicate mild, moderate or severe degrees of burden. Zarit, Orr and Zarit (1985) used a modification of the Lowenthal (1967) clinical questionnaire to study 29 older people with dementia and their primary caregivers. In 1985, the authors redesigned the Burden Interview, studying caregivers of relatives with Alzheimer's disease. Cronbach's alpha for the Burden Interview was 0.88 (Zarit, 1994).

Caregiver Burnout

Burnout was measured by scores on the Maslach Burnout Inventory (MBI) (Maslach & Jackson, 1986). The inventory consists of 22 items in three subscales: emotional exhaustion, personal accomplishment, and depersonalization. Because the instrument was designed to measure burnout in helping professionals, the MBI was modified in order to reflect instructions for family caregivers. This modification and subsequent psychometric validation was conducted by the researcher during the pilot work (described later in this chapter) in the summer of 1992 on an African-American caregiving population in the Greater New Orleans area using subjects (N=9) from the African-American church community.

The MBI indicated a high score on emotional exhaustion and depersonalization, and a low score on the personal adjustment scale for these pilot subjects (Maslach & Jackson, 1981). The MBI has established internal consistency reliability values using 1,000 professionals who provided care and assistance to others. Cronbach's

Alpha coefficient for the frequency subscales are as follows: emotional exhaustion (r=0.90), depersonalization (r=0.79), and personal accomplishment (r=0.71). The intensity scale has Alpha coefficients of r=0.87 for emotional exhaustion, r=0.76 for depersonalization, and r=0.73 for personal accomplishment. Test-retest reliability coefficients were obtained on 53 graduate students in social work. The frequency scale has a test-retest reliability across the three categories ranging from 0.60 to 0.82, and an intensity scale ranging from 0.53 to 0.69 (Maslach & Jackson, 1981).

Chronically Ill Frail Elderly

Chronically ill health status was determined using the Activities of Daily Living (ADL) Index (Katz, Ford, Moskowitz, Jackson & Jaffe, 1963) and the Mental Status Questionnaire (MSQ) designed by Kahn, Goldfarb, Pollack and Peck (1960). The ADL Index measures six activities of daily living functions in decreasing order of dependency (bathing, dressing, going to the toilet, transferring, continence and feeding). Using a Guttman scale, each item is given one point (Katz, et al., 1963). Reliability coefficients of 0.97 were established on a sample from the Fall River Sheltered Housing scale (Kane & Kane, 1981).

The MSQ measures impaired cognitive status such as that found in dementia. Two or more mistakes on the MSQ indicates dementia. The authors sampled 1,077 patients, aged 65 or older, in homes for the aged, nursing homes and state mental hospitals in New York City in 1958. The results showed that the MSQ was highly correlated with psychiatrists' clinical evaluations of the presence of cognitive impairment (Kahn, et al., 1960). Cronbach's alpha for the MSQ was 0.84 (Kane & Kane, 1981).

Health Services Utilization

Health services utilization was measured pre- and post-intervention by the caregiver completing the "Use of Care Program" section of the Caregiver Demographic Profile Form. The caregiver checked all of the service agencies used. The results were categorized as "yes" or "no" responses by the caregiver and summed for a total score.

Self-Directed Skills Model

The Self-Directed Skills (SDS) model was used as the intervention protocol that provided a systematic approach for processing family dynamics. The following family tools developed by Satir and Baldwin (1983) were used: making contact, family map of origin, paternal and maternal family maps, communication stances, wheel of influence, the iceberg, change process, family rules, self-mandala, and the self-esteem maintenance kit (see Appendix for copies of tools used in the study).

INTERVENTION PROTOCOL

Research participants were randomized into an experimental and control group using a table of random numbers. The researcher and/or research assistants met with each of the group participants for a total of 24 hours over a period of 12 sessions. The following protocol was implemented in this study.

Procedure for Experimental Group

Assessment Phase

During Sessions 1 and 2, the researcher contacted the experimental group's research participants and assisted the PFCs in completing the instrument packet and assessing the goals for change (pre-test).

Planning and Intervention Phase

During Session 3, the researcher completed the family of origin and paternal and maternal maps of experimental group participants (Satir, et al., 1991). Research participants also shared their family rules, and the researcher tapped the internal resources of the family caregiver (his/her feelings, yearnings and unfinished business), noting patterns and tracking, and weaving and reframing the interaction as necessary. The Satir tools and techniques that were used were: the iceberg, change process (transformation), map reading, metaphors, sculpting, and anchoring the new learnings.

During Session 4, the researcher reconnected with the participants and continued to establish rapport and build trust. The researcher continued to build on the process of emerged family data (from Session 3) by helping the experimental participants resolve present problems, yearnings, expectations, perceptions and feelings through increased self-esteem and self-care behaviors (see case study in this chapter for complete derivation).

The researcher continued to build on the content and process of the previous sessions during Sessions 5 and 6. Using the family map data, research participants verbalized their communication stances (blaming, placating, distracting, superreasonable) and their coping and stress patterns. The Satir tools used during Sessions 5 and 6 were reframing, map reading, the iceberg, and processing the new behaviors acquired by the PFCs.

Evaluation Phase

In Sessions 7 through 9, the researcher used the Satir Growth Paradigm to process the experimental participants' new behaviors (learnings), noting their congruent communication, self-care behaviors, and use of formal and informal health service agencies. The researcher also tapped the internal resources of the research participants, noting their new profile of the self and their relationship with the care recipient. The Satir tools used during the evaluation phase were the iceberg, change process, sculpting, tracking and weaving (see case study in this chapter).

Neither the researcher nor the research assistants had contact with the PFCs and care recipients during Sessions 10 and 11. During Session 12, the researcher readministered the research instrument packet to the experimental group participants (post-test).

The researcher's total contact hours with each experimental group participant was 24 hours. The researcher collected data for the Satir content and process by using handwritten notations of the caregivers' dialogue and the researcher's observations and by applying Satir's principles.

The researcher analyzed the interactions of the PFC for themes and phrases indicative of the Satir definitions of enmeshment, caregiver burden, the potential for caregiver burnout and self-esteem messages. The themes were defined as generalizations or family patterns that were characterized by the Satir principles in the family maps, communication stances, and the wheel of influence. Analysis of the content and process provided the researcher with qualitative data that reflected the pre- and post-intervention states of the experimental and control group research participants. These qualitative data are presented in Chapter IV.

Case Study--Experimental Group

The following case study is presented as a prototype for the PFCs who were in the experimental group of this research study. The following format was used: the dialogue is presented in the left column of the page and the researcher's interpretations/ comments regarding the Satir paradigm are presented in the right column. The names were changed for the purpose of confidentiality. The context of the caregiving situation was explored through the researcher questioning the PFCs regarding family relationships. Family of origin, maternal and parental maps, family rules, communication stances, wheel of influence, the iceberg, self-esteem maintenance kit, and the mandala were used to assess and promote internal change in the PFC.

Dialogue	Interpretations/Comments

(Sessions 3 through 6)

RESEARCHER: Thanks, Mrs. Johnson, for agreeing to participate in my research study. I am a doctoral student in nursing at The University of Iowa. I am looking at family relationships, communication, and influences, and how you relate to others as a primary family caregiver (PFC) of an elderly family member.	The researcher used the experiental teaching-learning cycle as a guide to collect data for the research study (see Figure 2). *Making contact* with the PFC and care recipient. The researcher explained the research plan and what was expected of Mrs. Johnson and the care recipient. The goal of the model was to add on self-growth patterns (Satir, et al, 1991).
MRS. JOHNSON: I am happy to help. I have been caring for my grandmother for nearly a year.	Mrs. Johnson agreed to participate in the study.
RESEARCHER: The plan is that you share with me your caregiving process and we will work through things that surface so as to see if there are changes in your responses to the pre- and post-questionnaires.	The researcher *connected* with the PFC so as to collect data on family and caregiving and to provide feedback.

MRS. JOHNSON: This study seems to be a rather involved research plan.

RESEARCHER: Yes, it is. Remember it's 24 contact hours. We have 18 more hours to go. I will not meet with you during the tenth and eleventh sessions. We will redo the questionnaires and terminate.

The 24-hour contact time frame was designed to enhance self-esteem so as to allow for review of the PFC's caregiving, rethinking and processing self-esteem messages and to decrease enmeshment with family members, decrease caregiving burntout, and to increase use of health service agencies.

MRS. JOHNSON: Well, let's get started.

[Mrs. Johnson and the researcher completed the family maps, the wheel of influence, the family rules and the communication stances of father, mother, care recipient and herself (PFC).]

The researcher completes the family map (3 generations) on the Johnson family using the Satir tools (family maps, wheel of influencing and family rules) (see Figures 4, 5, 6 and 7 at the end of this discussion). The researcher shared patterns in family maps that are indicative of caregiving behaviors and familial communication patterns that emerge with the PFC.

The researcher lets the PFC continue to share her caregiving so as to provide a safe and familiar climate.

(The researcher continues to observe and process the family data.)

PFCs
Father: Blamer
Mother: Placator
Care Recipient: Blamer and
super-reasonable

PFC: Placator

The PFC was influenced by her
mother and grandmother.

RESEARCHER: Mrs. Johnson,
share a typical day with me.

MRS. JOHNSON: I get up in
the morning and take care of
my family (breakfast, fix lunch
for the children and my
husband, get things together to
care for my grandmother). My
husband and daughter help me
with caring for my
grandmother.

Sharing a typical day was a
technique used by the
researcher to get the PFC
talking about caregiving
(observing and processing the
data helped the researcher
rebuild the self-esteem of the
caregiving and decrease
enmeshment cues that surfaces.
Exploring caregiver burden and
the potential for burnout were
also assessed and validated.

My husband takes care of the
business, such as running
errands, arranging doctor visits,
paying the bills, check on her
(grandmother's) home,
gardening. This really takes the
pressure off of me. My
daughter helps me in the
evening to walk my
grandmother.

It's a funny thing. My
grandmother is a very proud
woman. She never wanted for
anything. Now that she is in
failing health, she has become

less vain. She does not look into the mirror. She has gotten darker. She doesn't even want to wash her face. This, to me, is strange. It is hard at times caring for her and seeing her health fail her but the caring I have for her is unspeakable joy. She, in her own way, loves me.

I remember how she would help me when I was young. I would tell her what I needed before I told my parents. I was the ugly duckling in my family. My sisters got all the attention from my parents. I was sensitive and fearful of my father. My grandmother would rescue me and stand up to him. I really think back on this and the feelings I get are love, kindness, warmth and acceptance. She and I are very close. There is nothing I would not do for her. My feelings are easily hurt. I am fearful most of the time. I always want to please others.

RESEARCHER: Tell me about these feelings of always wanting to please others.

The researcher wanted the PFC's communication pattern to emerge so as to have her hear how she sees herself.

MRS. JOHNSON: Well, in my family, there was no togetherness. My family would leave me out of things. I looked up to my two older sisters. I am very close to my brother. When there were problems, I usually gave in to what my family wanted.

RESEARCHER: How did this make you feel?

Emerging the feelings of the PFC so as to have her self-reflect on the family data she has shared with the researcher.

MRS. JOHNSON: I felt like nothing. My mother usually felt sorry for herself. I guess I must have inherited this from her. Sometimes I feel sorry for myself. I cannot remember how long I have been feeling this way.

RESEARCHER: Let's get to know you. I have a diagram I call "The Iceberg" in which you look at yourself in levels. [The researcher shows the iceberg diagram to Mrs. Johnson.]

The researcher was helping the PFC get to know herself mre intimately. Using the iceberg, as designed by Satir, to begin the process of transformation. The PFC would look at her inner experiences and determine how she relates to others and herself (Satir, et al., 1991).

Mrs. Johnson, describe yourself to me using the diagram, starting with the "I am" section and proceeding upward.

[As the PFC talked, the researcher wrote, observed, and processed the data.]

MRS. JOHNSON: "I am"--I am sensitive and frustrated at times with my grandmother's failing health. I get so angry.

Satir and her colleagues (1991) believed that working through the iceberg brings the persor (PFC) "into more self-integration and congruence" (p. 173).

Yearnings: I want to be able to speak up for myself and not feel guilty when I am angry.

Expectations: I want to be able to ask for what I want so that I can feel relieved and accepted.

Perceptions: I believe I can be less sensitive when I am confronted by others in a negative manner.

Feelings: I feel inadequate and unable to defend myself so I stay quiet when people are upset with me.

Behavior: I try to please others, especially my husband and grandmother. I cry to myself a lot.

RESEARCHER: You feel inadequate and have low self-esteem. You tend to placate to your husband and others.

MRS. JOHNSON: Yes, I usually avoid conflict. I have high blood pressure, headaches, and left leg pain. I am even-tempered and sweet. I know I let people walk all over me. I have gained so much weight over the last two years. I still cry a lot. I hold things in and I get depressed easily.

The researcher interprets the iceberg information to the PFC.

Mrs. Johnson agreed with the researcher that she tended to be a placator and had low self-esteem.

RESEARCHER: Let's see how much you know about yourself. I have the mandala, which is a way of ranking your universal parts. (The researcher explains the mandala to Mrs. Johnson.)

Mrs. Johnson ranks the mandala as follows:

1. Nutritional
2. Physical
3. Emotional
4. Intellectual
5. Contextual
6. Spiritual
7. Interactional
8. Sensual

[Sessions 7 through 9]

RESEARCHER: You have the internal resources to change your view of yourself. Let's use the self-esteem maintenance kit to give you some information on how to rebuild your self-esteem.

[Researcher gives Mrs. Johnson the self-esteem kit after relating (lecturette style) the purpose and how to use the kit to provide a foundation for exploring and building her self-esteem.]

The researcher used the mandala to continue to integrate the PFC's image of herself. Satir, et al. (1991) believed that the mandala interrelates the internal resources of the self. The shift of the internal resources increased the PFC's awareness so as to provide self-support, acceptance and a new way to provide quality caregiving.

Mrs. Johnson's concept of herself was validated by her responses to the mandala and her knowledge of her well-being.

The self-esteem maintenance kit was used as a "symbolic metaphor to increase people's sense of inner resources and self-esteem. The idea is to take greater responsibility and be connected to our deeper source of wisdom" (Satir, 1991, p. 298).

[The researcher then uses the iceberg, mandala and self-esteem kit to relook at Mrs. Johnson's view of herself.]

RESEARCHER: Mrs. Johnson, let's reuse the iceberg and mandala to access your understanding of how you have grown during the SDS nursing intervention sessions.

The researcher used the mandala and the iceberg again to reinforce learning and to have the PFC process her own self-directed skills, thus transforming dysfunctional material (de-enmeshment process) into self-acceptance and increasing self-esteem. Mrs. Johnson was able to process her growth and was able to use humor to look at her self-growth patterns over the research session.

[Mrs. Johnson smiles.]

MRS. JOHNSON: You know, I have seen growth in me." My mandala looks good to me:

1. Interactional
2. Spiritual
3. Emotional
4. Intellectual
5. Physical
6. Nutritional
7. Contextual
8. Sensual

See, my communication has improved. I can understand my talking to others. I use structure to an advantage. My time is accounted for during the day. I am more cheerful and confident. I take more risks with myself as a caregiver and wife. I am aware of my ability to make choices; therefore, I am open to new possibilities. I have come to the opinion that my family did the best they could do with what they were given to live with. I see the influence my family had on me. My "iceberg" is very different now.

I am: I am able to tell others what I am feeling right then and there. I don't hold things in any longer. I don't have the heaviness in my chest, headaches, and sinus trouble.

The researcher provided Mrs. Johnson with the choice of new possibilities in caregiving. Mrs. Johnson was able to experience growth and change with the Satir Processing Model.

Yearnings: I have been unleashed. I don't know what I have become, but I know I am different. You don't know how much I have held in for years. I *expect* to stand on my two feet. I know how far to go with my husband and my grand-mother. I still at times placate. I am aware of how I am communicating with others. I *perceive* that I can develop my own way of relating to people. I am aware of how I feel on the inside. I *feel* good about how I communicate. I just let the past take care of the past. I can move on the future, but I am participating in the present. Did you hear what I said? I think you have unleashed or created a monster (smile). I am different; I have changed. My *behavior* is interesting. I am aware of what I say to others and how I say it. I won't get trapped again. I am much happier. I know my self-esteem has improved. It is good to know how I developed and how this development affected my relating to others. My grandmother's care has improved. She is much sicker, but she is not a burden to me; I am not tired either.

RESEARCHER: What else do you do to manage your caregiving?

MRS. JOHNSON: I take time out for me now. I listen to music and relax now.

[12th session--Researcher readministered the questionnaires.]

Post-intervention questionnaires were done to validate change in Mrs. Johnson's self-esteem, enmeshment, burden, burnout, and health services utilization.

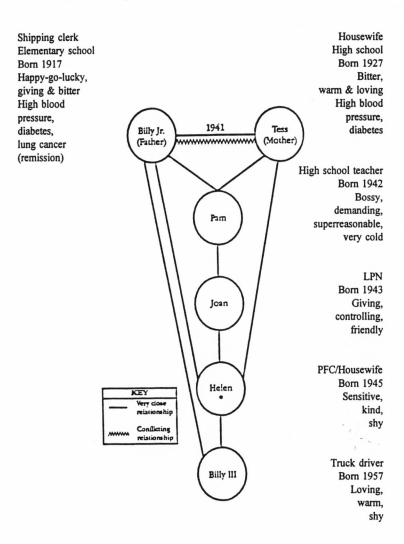

Shipping clerk
Elementary school
Born 1917
Happy-go-lucky,
giving & bitter
High blood
pressure,
diabetes,
lung cancer
(remission)

Housewife
High school
Born 1927
Bitter,
warm & loving
High blood
pressure,
diabetes

1941

Billy Jr.
(Father)

Tess
(Mother)

High school teacher
Born 1942
Bossy,
demanding,
superreasonable,
very cold

Pam

LPN
Born 1943
Giving,
controlling,
friendly

Joan

PFC/Housewife
Born 1945
Sensitive,
kind,
shy

Helen

KEY

——— Very close
relationship

wwww Conflicting
relationship

Truck driver
Born 1957
Loving,
warm,
shy

Billy III

Figure 4. Mrs. Johnson's Family of Origin Map

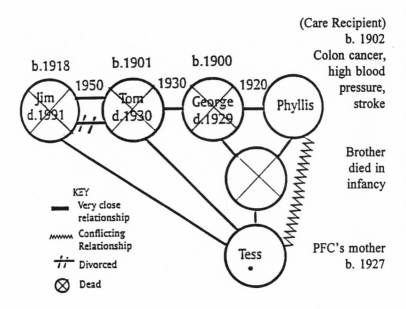

NOTES: • Grandmother, Phyllis did not want to be grandmother or mother. Tess was raised by a friend of the family.
   • George, 1st husband of Phyllis, was shot by her.
   • Tom, 2nd husband of Phyllis, died of emphysema in 1930.
   • Jim, 3rd husband of Phyllis, died in 1991 of a heart attack. He and Phyllis were divorced in 1970. This divorce left Phyllis very bitter and angry.
   • Tess and Jim had a very close relationship.

Figure 5. Mrs. Johnson's Maternal Family Map

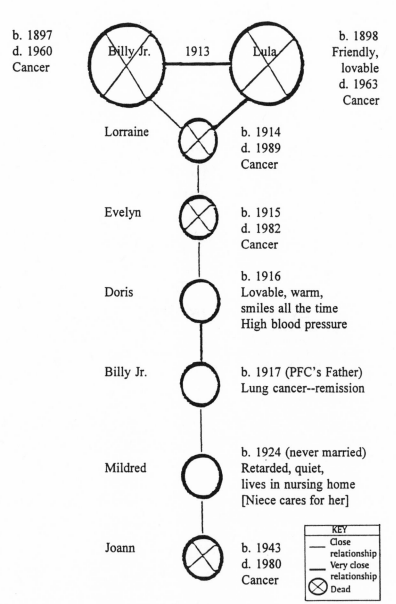

Figure 6. Mrs. Johnson's Paternal Family Map

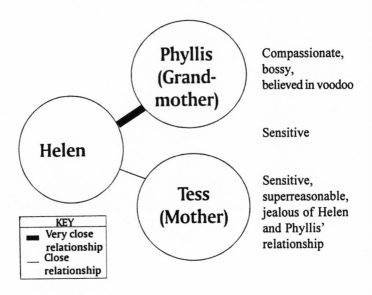

Figure 7. Mrs. Johnson's Wheel of Influence

When asked about family rules, Mrs. Johnson expressed the following comments to the researcher:

1. We had no rules. Mama was boss of the house.
2. Daddy was boss of Mama.
3. Everybody was an individiual and we did our own thing.
4. Don't cause the family problems.
5. Daddy believed in a happy family--eat, drink and be merry. Let the good times roll.
6. Life is easy if you get along with people.
7. Daddy always had the last say in our house.
8. Grandmother (Phyllis) had the last say in family decisions.

Procedure for Control Group

Assessment Phase

During Sessions 1 and 2, the researcher contacted the control group research participants and assisted the PFCs in completing the research questionnaires.

Planning and Intervention Phase

A research assistant (RA) was assigned to the control group during the planning and intervention phase of the research process (Session 3 through Session 9). Each RA was instructed as to how to carry out the research process with the control group participants. The goal for this phase was to implement a friendly visit (one-to-one process) with the PFC. The context of the visit was predicated on the interactions between the PFC and the research assistant.

The research assistant was instructed to not talk about family relationships, self-growth, and self-management skills with the PFCs. The care recipients received blood pressure checks and one-to-one interaction with the research assistant. The purpose of the control group was not to receive the experimental variable (the Satir paradigm); the RAs were only to do friendly visits. As in the experimental group, the RAs had no contact with the PFCs and care recipients during Sessions 10 and 11.

Evaluation Phase

During Session 12, the researcher readministered the research instrument packet to the control group participants (post-test). The research assistant's total contact hours with each control group participant was 14 hours, while the researcher's contact was 10 hours, thus totally 24 hours (the same amount of time spent with the experimental group).

DATA COLLECTION AND ANALYSIS

The researcher analyzed the quantitative data by using the Statistical Package for Social Science (SPSS-PC) (Norusis, 1990), chi-square, freqencies, percent and paired t-tests. Using the Satir paradigm, qualitative exemplars from experimental group's PFCs were evaluated in relation to burden, burnout, enmeshment, self-esteem and health services utilization. Demographic data were displayed in appropriate graphs and tables.

The paired t-test measured the mean differences between any pre and post scores for the experimental and control groups in levels of self-esteem, enmeshment, burden and burnout. The hypotheses were tested using both quantitative and qualitative data analysis.

HUMAN SUBJECTS APPROVAL

Approval was given by The University of Iowa Human Subjects Committee A, and informed consent was obtained from all participants.

PILOT STUDY

To calculate power for the major study on African-American PFCs, the researcher randomly assigned nine PFCs from a sample of 35 to control (5) and experimental (4) groups from the Greater New Orleans area. Only nine PFCs participated in the study because 26 PFCs did not meet the research selection criteria.

The criteria for selection of the PFCs were based on the mental status and activities of daily living limitations of the care recipient; the PFC caregiving load of 100 percent; and the PFC's willingness to participate in the study for three months.

The data used for the power analysis of pre-test and post-test differences of PFCs in both the control and experimental groups showed no significant differences between the two groups. The care recipients also showed no significant differences in the pre-test and post-test results on mental status and activities of daily living inventories.

Therefore, to achieve a 70 percent chance of detecting group differences of one unit in change from pre-intervention scores for enmeshment, the researcher needed 24 subjects in each group. To achieve an 80 percent change of detecting change from baseline, 30 subjects were needed in each group. Self-esteem data showed that in order to achieve a 70 percent chance of detecting a difference of one unit change from baseline, 13 subjects in each group would be needed, and an 80 percent chance in detecting a two unit change from baseline required 11 subjects in each group. The researcher assumed that the PFCs' burden and burnout differences from baseline would be captured on the basis of enmeshment and self-esteem.

The researcher modified the selection criteria for PFCs and care recipients for the major study from 100 percent total care of the frail homebound elderly relative to those persons who provided 60 to 75 percent of daily care to frail elderly relatives. Additionally, the research time frame was changed from a three-month period to a one-month period and, finally, the sample population was selected from local African-American community churches within a 100-mile radius of New Orleans rather than from African-American churches within the Greater New Orleans metropolitan area. It was also determined that 30 PFCs and care recipients would be needed per group to provide supportive data to evaluate the research purposes and hypotheses.

SUMMARY

The study used an experimental design to test a nursing intervention model, SDS, by measuring differences in its effectiveness between the experimental and control groups on levels of self-esteem, enmeshment, burden, burnout and health services utilization. The intervention protocol measured both pre- and post-effects of the PFC's burnout in caring for a frail homebound elderly relative. The care recipients' physical limitations and mental status were also measured.

There were 60 PFCs and 60 care recipients who agreed to participate in the study. The sample was randomly assigned into

30 PFCs and care recipients for the experimental and control groups, respectively. The Satir paradigm was used by the researcher to guide the structured interviews for the experimental group, and the control group received friendly visits from research assistants.

IV

Data Analysis

This chapter presents the results of quantitative and qualitative analyses of the data and begins with a detailed description of the demographic characteristics of the care recipients and PFCs. The chapter also presents the study findings in response to the research questions and hypotheses.

CHARACTERISTICS OF THE SAMPLE OF CARE RECIPIENTS

Demographic Characteristics

Subjects in both the experimental and control groups were African-Americans who were predominantly Protestants, laborers and married females (see Table 1). Table 2 shows that the majority of the sample was literate. Although 21.7 percent had no schooling, 36.7 percent of the care recipients had an elementary education, 27 percent had some education or had completed high school, and 15 percent had some college education or had completed college.

Figure 8 shows the age distribution of care recipients. Seventy-seven percent of the subjects were 60 to 79 years old and 23.33 percent were from 80 to 105 years of age. The mean age for the control group was 74 years and 75 years for the experimental group.

As Table 3 shows, the relationship to the PFC was predominantly that of husband to wife (20% control and 43% experimental); wives were 20 percent of the care recipients in the control group, but only 10 percent in the experimental. Twenty percent of the control care

Table 1. Demographic Characteristics of the Care Recipient

Characteristics	Control Group (N=30)		Experimental Group (N=30)		Combined Groups (N=60)	
	No.	%	No.	%	Frequency	%
Sex (X^2=1.71; df=1; p=0.190[NS])						
Female	20	66.67	15	50.00	--	--
Male	10	33.33	15	50.00	--	--
Marital Status (X^2=3.39; df=3; p=0.335[NS])						
Single	--	--	1	3.33	--	--
Married	17	56.67	17	56.67	--	--
Divorced	--	--	2	6.67	--	--
Widowed	13	43.33	10	33.33	--	--
Usual Occupation						
Laborer	--	--	--	--	52	86.70
Technical	--	--	--	--	2	3.30
Professional	--	--	--	--	6	10.00

Table 1 (continued)

Characteristics	Control Group (N=30)		Experimental Group (N=30)		Combined Groups (N=60)	
	No.	%	No.	%	Frequency	%
Religious Affiliation (X^2=0.35; df=1; p=0.554[NS])						
Protestant	28	93.33	29	96.67	--	--
Catholic	2	6.67	1	3.33	--	--

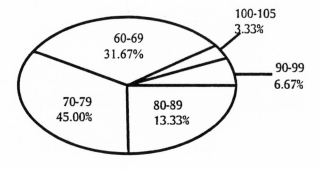

Figure 8. Age Distribution of Care Recipients

Table 2. Care Recipient's Educational Preparation by Frequencies and Percent

	Frequency	%
No Schooling	13	21.70
Elementary School	22	36.70
Some High School	10	16.60
Finished High School	6	10.00
Some College	5	8.30
Completed 4 or More Years of College	4	6.70

Table 3. Chi-Square Results With Frequencies and Percents of Care Recipient's Family Relationships by Groups

	Control Group (N=30)		Experimental Group (N=30)	
	No.	%	No.	%
Family Relationship (X^2=13.71; p=0.133[NS])				
Husband	6	20.00	13	43.33
Wife	6	20.00	3	10.00
Sister	2	6.67	--	--
Daughter	2	--	1	3.33
Son	--	--	1	3.33
Aunt	3	10.00	--	--
Uncle	1	3.33	--	--
Mother	6	20.00	9	30.00
Father	2	6.67	--	--
Other (Grandmother)	2	6.67	3	10.00

recipients were mothers, as compared to 30 percent in the experimental group. A chi-square analysis was computed on the care recipient's relationship to the PFC and was found to be non-significant. A greater (but nonstatistically significant) percentage of the care recipients in the experimental group were husbands and mothers (73%) than the control group (40%) (X^2=13.71, df=9, p=0.133).

The majority of the care recipients had been homebound for over three years (56.67%) (X^2=5.60, df=2, p=0.062) (see Table 4). There was no association noted between group membership and length of time homebound as tested by X^2.

Figure 9 graphically displays the care recipient's years of being homebound in relation to years of family caregiving by control and experimental groups. Although Table 4 indicates a nonsignificant X^2 of 0.062 for the care recipient's length of time for being homebound, according to group, the p value is close to significant. Consequentially, in the control group, the caregivers had provided care for more than three years, whereas in the experimental group, more caregivers had provided care for less than one year.

Table 4. Chi-Square Results of Care Recipient's Length of Time Being Homebound

	Control (N=30)		Experimental (N=30)		Combined (N=60)	
	No.	%	No.	%	No.	%
6 months - 1 year	1	3.30	7	23.30	8	13.33
13 months - 3 years	9	15.00	9	15.00	18	30.00
Over 3 years	20	66.67	14	46.67	34	56.67

X^2=5.60; df=2; p=0.062

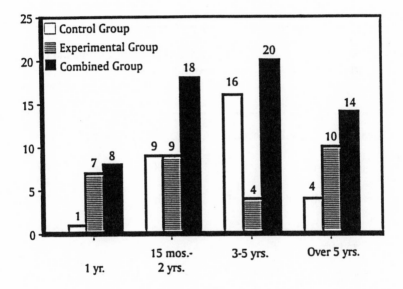

Figure 9. Number of Care Recipients and Years of Family Caregiving (N=60)

A chi-square was performed on care recipients' reasons for being homebound according to group (see Table 5). Care recipients who were both disoriented and physically ill (47% control group and 50% experimental group) resulted in a chi square value of $X^2=0.23$, df=2 and p=0.889, indicating that there was no association between the control and experimental groups on these variables.

Table 5. Care Recipient's Reasons for Being Homebound by Control and Experimental Group

	Control Group (N=30)		Experimental Group (N=30)	
	No.	%	No.	%
Reason for Being Homebound ($X^2=0.23$; df=2; p=0.889[NS])				
Disoriented	3	10.00	2	6.67
Physically Ill	13	43.33	13	43.33
Both Disoriented and Physically Ill	14	46.67	15	50.00

Table 6 shows the care recipient's reason for being homebound according to the length of time being homebound. The results indicated that the majority of the care recipients in both groups were disoriented and physically ill, and had been homebound for over three years, thus reflecting a predominantly chronically-ill population of care recipients.

Table 6. Reason for Being Homebound by Length of Time Being Homebound (Care Recipient) (N=60)

	Disoriented	Physically Ill	Disoriented & Physically Ill
6 Months - 1 Year	0	4	4
13 Months - 3 Years	2	7	9
Over 3 Years	3	15	16

RESULTS OF CARE RECIPIENTS' INSTRUMENTS

Mental Status Questionnaire (MSQ)

Status of the care recipients (N=60) was measured using the Mental Status Questionnaire (MSQ) and the Activities of Daily Living (ADL) Index. In this study, Cronbach's alpha was .94 (pre-test) and .96 (post-test) for the MSQ. Paired t-tests were conducted on the means of the care recipients in both control and experimental groups to evaluate change over time. The mean score for the MSQ increased for the control group from 3.80 pre-intervention to 3.96 post-intervention. The mean score for the experimental group was 4.87 pre-intervention and decreased to 4.67 post-intervention. This difference may be attributed to the contact time and sharing the PFCs and care recipients had with the researcher. Although the care recipients tended to become more frail over the course of the study, a statistically significant difference in mental status was not found from pre- to post-test (see Table 7 for the mean change score for MSQ). High scores on the MSQ indicated more impairment.

Mean differences between the post- and pre-intervention evaluation scores of the MSQ for the care recipients were not significantly

Table 7. *Mean Scores for Evaluation of Status of Care Recipient Pre-and Post-Intervention by Group*

	Control Group (N=30)		Experimental Group (N=30)	
	Pre Mean	Post Mean	Pre Mean	Post Mean
Mental Status	3.80	10.00	4.87	4.67
Questionnaire	(3.92)	(4.26)	(4.07)	(4.32)
Activities of	15.40	15.60	15.30	15.67
Daily Living	(2.77)	(3.17)	(2.48)	(2.56)
(Standard Deviation)				

different (control group X=0.17, t=0.52, p=0.6046; experimental group X=0.20, t=4.75, p=0.5727) (see Table 8). No significant differences were found in the mean change in the status of care recipients in the control versus experimental groups, as shown in Table 9 (control group X=0.17; experimental group X=-0.20, t=0.78, p=0.4418). Therefore, mental status of the care recipients did not differ significantly with respect to the control and experimental groups over time.

Activities of Daily Living (ADL) Index

Cronbach's alpha for ADL Index was .85 (pre-test) and .90 (post-test) for this sample. The mean score of the care recipients on the ADL Index increased over the course of the study from 15.4 to 15.6 for the control group pre- and post-intervention, respectively. For the experimental group, the mean score increased from 15.3 pre-intervention to 15.67 post-intervention. The ADL scores increased over the course of the study as the care recipients became more frail. The ADL Index mean differences between the post- versus the pre-evaluation scores were X=0.23, t=0.47 and p=0.6208 for the control group. The

Table 8. Mean Differences Between Post- Versus Pre-Evaluation Scores

	Control Group (N=30)			Experimental Group (N=30)		
	Mean	t	p-value	Mean	t	p-value
Mental Status Questionnaire	0.17	0.52	0.6046	-0.20	-4.75	0.5725
Activities of Daily Living	0.23	0.47	0.6208	0.33	0.93	0.3577

Table 9. Care Recipients' Mean Scores Change in Control Versus Experimental Groups

	Control	Experimental	t	p-value
Mental Status Questionnaire	0.17	-0.20	0.78	0.4418
Activities of Daily Living	0.23	0.33	-0.17	0.8654

experimental group's scores were X=0.33, t=0.93 and p=0.3577 (see Table 9). These data showed that there were no significant differences found between the control and experimental groups' ADL Index scores over the course of the study (see Tables 7, 8 and 9).

Summary

In summary, care recipients in both the control and experimental groups were similar on demographic characteristics. The data also showed that there were no significant differences in the Mental Status Questionnaire and Activity of Daily Living Index for subjects in the experimental and control groups before and after the SDS intervention model. The scores on the MSQ and ADL Index indicated that the care recipients became more frail over the course of the study. Although the MSQ scores of the care recipients in the experimental group decreased after SDS intervention, the results showed the groups were similar at baseline and after SDS intervention.

CHARACTERISTICS OF THE SAMPLE OF PRIMARY FAMILY CAREGIVERS (PFCs)

Demographic Characteristics

Characteristics of the 60 PFCs in this study were as follows. There were 46 females (76.65%) and 14 males (23.35%) in the study. The religious preferences of the sample were Protestant (96.65%) and Catholic (3.35%). Forty PFCs were between the ages of 60 to 79 (66.67%) (see Figure 10). The mean age was 60 years for the control group and 61 years for the experimental group. Almost all subjects were related to the care recipient as wife (60%), daughter (46.67%) or husband (36.66%) (see Table 10).

Eighty-three percent of the PFCs were laborers and a majority were literate: 26.7 percent had an educational level of some elementary schooling, while 51.7 percent had attended high school (see Table 11). The demographic data for the PFCs are summarized in Tables 10 and 11.

RESULTS OF CAREGIVERS' CHECKLIST

The PFCs responded to a checklist on the number of responsibilities they held and what health service agencies were utilized while providing care to a frail elderly relative (see Tables 14 and 15). The PFCs checked as many of the responses as applied to their situation, thus the total of the percentages is greater than 100%.

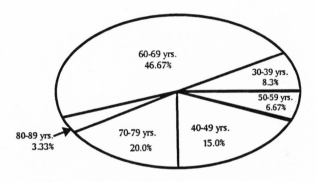

Figure 10. Age Distribution of Primary Family Caregivers

Table 10. Demographic Characteristics of Primary Family Caregiver

Characteristic	Control Group (N=30)		Experimental Group (N=30)	
	No.	%	No.	%
Sex (X^2=1.49; df=1; p=0.222^{NS})				
Female	21	70.00	25	83.33
Male	9	30.00	5	16.67
Religious Affiliation (X^2 = 2.07; df = 1; p = 0.150^{NS})				
Protestant	28	93.33	30	100.00
Male	2	6.67	--	--
Marital Status (X^2 = 4.31; df = 5; p = 0.506^{NS})				
Single	3	10.00	1	3.33
Married	18	60.00	24	79.97
Divorced	3	10.00	2	6.67
Widowed	5	16.67	3	10.00
Other (Common-Law Wife)	1	3.33	--	--
Family Relationship (X^2 = 12.66; df = 8; p = 0.124^{NS})				
Husband	7	23.33	4	13.33
Wife	5	16.67	13	43.33
Sister	2	6.67	--	--
Brother	1	3.33	--	--
Daughter	5	16.67	9	30.00
Son	3	10.00	1	3.33
Aunt	1	3.33	--	--
Mother	2	6.67	--	--
Other (Niece, Granddaughter)	4	13.33	3	10.00

Table 11. PFC's Level of Education and Usual Occupation

Characteristic	Frequency	%
Education		
No Schooling	3	5.00
Elementary School	16	26.70
Some High School	21	35.00
Finished High School	10	16.70
Some College	5	8.30
Completed 4 or More Years of College	5	8.30
Usual Occupation		
Laborer	50	83.40
Technical	5	8.30
Professional	5	8.30

In general, as seen in Table 12, the PFC assumed total responsibility for the care recipient. The PFCs in both groups assumed greater responsibilities for the care recipient in shopping, transportation, problem solving, meal preparation, housekeeping, companionship and leisure time. Given these heavy responsibilities, the use of formal health care service agencies would seem logical as a measure to decrease everyday caregiving hassles; however, as seen in Table 13, the most frequently used service category was family members (83.3%). Control group PFCs used health service agencies more frequently than experimental group PFCs, although chi-square analysis revealed no significant association between group membership and use of health service agencies (see Table 13). The results indicated that the social worker at the hospital and other service contacts, such as hair stylists, physical therapists and community care workers, had a slight impact on the PFCs' caregiving behaviors.

Table 12. *Frequency Table of Responsibilities Assumed by*
         Caregivers

Responsibility	Control Group (N=30)		Experimental Group (N=30)	
	No.	%	No.	%
Personal Care	23	76.7	25	83.3
Financial Support	15	50.0	18	60.0
Housing	25	83.3	25	83.3
Personal Affairs	24	80.0	28	93.3
Shopping	30	100.0	29	96.7
Agency Services	19	63.3	25	83.3
Transportation	28	93.3	29	96.7
Locating Nursing Home	23	76.7	27	90.0
Problem Solving	24	80.0	27	90.0
Meal Preparation	28	93.3	27	90.0
Housekeeping	29	96.7	28	93.3
Companionship	27	90.0	29	96.7
Leisure Time	26	86.7	28	93.3
Other	--	--	1	3.3

The above findings also suggest that this sample of PFCs did not use formal health care agencies. Other family members were the most frequently named category that assisted them in caregiving. The control and experimental groups were similar with respect to sex, age, religious affiliation, marital status, caregiving responsibilities and health services utilization.

*Table 13. Frequency Table of Health Service Utilization by Control and Experimental Groups Pre- and Post-Intervention**

Health Service	Control Group (N=30)		Experimental Group (N=30)		X^2	p-value
	No.	%	No.	%		
Adult Day Care	1	1.67	--	--	1.02	0.313
Short Term Nursing Home Stay	3	10.00	--	--	3.16	0.076
Home Health Nurse	13	43.33	12	40.00	0.07	0.793
Nurse Aide	16	53.33	10	33.33	2.44	0.118
Home Health Care	1	3.33	--	--	1.02	0.313
Personal Care	1	3.33	--	--	1.02	0.313
Homemaker Chore	2	6.67	--	--	2.07	0.150
Live-In Companion	--	--	--	--	--	--
Respite Care	--	--	--	--	--	--
Hospice Care	2	6.67	--	--	2.07	0.150
Family Members	25	83.33	25	83.33	--	1.000
Social Worker at Hospital	10	33.33	4	13.33	3.35	0.067
Area Agency on Aging	1	3.33	--	--	1.02	0.313

Table 13 continued

Health Service	Control Group (N=30)		Experimental Group (N=30)		X^2	p-value
	No.	%	No.	%		
State Agencies on Aging	1	3.33	--	--	1.02	0.313
Retired Senior Volunteer Program	1	3.33	1	3.33	--	1.000
Members of Your Church	6	20.00	4	13.33	0.48	0.488
Visiting Nurses Association	2	6.67	3	10.00	0.22	0.640
Other	--	--	4	13.00	4.29	0.038

*Pre- and post-data were identical.

QUANTITATIVE ANALYSIS

Organization of Analysis

The quantitative analysis of the findings about PFCs in this study was organized with reference to the t-test scores for evaluation of self-esteem, cohesion, adaptability, enmeshment, and burden and burnout in the PFC and the mean changes in the control versus experimental groups. The results are presented in response to the four research hypotheses and the discussion of the results concludes with a response to the research question. The dependent measures were caregiver burden, family adaptability and cohesion scale, caregiver burnout, self-esteem scale and a checklist of health services utilization. A t-test was done to assess control and experimental group differences at baseline for self-esteem, cohesion, adaptability, and caregiver burden and burnout. The results show that the PFCs in the experimental and control groups were similar at baseline on all variables (see Table 14). The Cronbach's alpha coefficients of the instruments used in the study for PFCs are as follows in Table 15.

HYPOTHESIS RESULTS

Hypothesis 1

Hypothesis 1: Subjects in the experimental group will report an increased level of self-esteem after administration of the SDS intervention compared to subjects in the control group.

Self-Esteem Scale

The results of the self-esteem scale were divided into two subscales (high and low) in evaluating the PFC's level of self-esteem. Self-esteem, as defined by Rosenberg (1979), has two broad aspects (cognitive and evaluative). Cognitive aspects of self-esteem include beliefs about various aspects of one's self such as body image, social identity, values, abilities and traits. The evaluative aspect of self-esteem consists of the positive and negative feelings one is aware of about one's self.

Table 14. T-Test Differences Between PFCs in Control and Experimental Groups at Baselines on Self-Esteem, Cohesion, Adaptability, Burden and Burnout

Variable	Control Group		Experimental Group		T-Test	p-value
	Mean	Standard Deviation	Mean	Standard Deviation		
Self-Esteem	25.23	2.30	24.70	1.89	0.98	0.3312
FACES II						
Cohesion	54.33	9.51	52.87	8.97	0.61	0.5414
Adaptability	46.60	8.40	46.06	9.73	0.23	0.8210
Burden	40.87	21.32	47.40	18.22	-1.28	0.2071
Burnout						
Emotion Exhaustion	35.57	14.07	40.10	11.66	-1.36	0.1796
Depersonalization	5.57	6.37	5.70	6.04	-0.08	0.9340
Personal Accomplishment	27.13	4.93	27.67	4.53	-0.44	0.6643

*Table 15. Cronbach's Alpha Coefficients of PFCs for Study Instruments
(N=60)*

Instrument	Pre-Test	Post-Test
Self-Esteem		
High	.87	.82
Low	.81	.86
FACES II		
Cohesion	.92	.90
Adaptability	.80	.81
Burden	.93	.93
Burnout		
Emotional Exhaustion	.85	.97
Depersonalization	.71	.71
Personal Accomplishment	.17	.48

Rosenberg (1979) characterized a person as having high self-esteem
when he considers himself a person of worth and has respect for
himself. The person is able to recognize his own faults and appreciate
his own merits. Low self-esteem, as defined by Rosenberg (1979),
means that a person lacks self-respect and considers himself unworthy,
inadequate and inefficient.

Therefore, the self-esteem data were analyzed on a 10-item scale in
which the respondents rated statements as agreement or disagreement
(5 negative and 5 positive). The responses were scored from "strongly
agree" (4) to "strongly disagree" (1). The possible scores ranged from
10 to 40. High scores indicated high self-esteem.

The high scores pre- and post-intervention for the control group
were 16.3 and 16.1, respectively, and 15.2 and 17.5, respectively, for
the experimental group (see Table 16). The low scores pre- and post-
intervention for the control group were 9.0 and 8.1, respectively, and
9.5 (pre-intervention) and 7.2 (post-intervention for the experimental
group. These data show that self-esteem of the PFCs in the experimental
group increased after the SDS intervention was administered. The

self-esteem of the PFCs in the control group decreased over the course of the study.

Table 16. Self-Esteem Mean Scores for Evaluation of Primary Family Caregivers

Variable	Control Group (N=30)		Experimental Group (N=30)	
	Pre	Post	Pre	Post
Self-Esteem				
High	16.3	16.1	15.2	17.5
	(2.58)	(2.17)	(2.81)	(1.9)
Low	9.0	8.1	9.5	7.2
	(3.14)	(2.79)	(2.28)	(2.11)
(Standard Deviation)				

The paired t-test results showed no statistically significant differences for the high and low levels of self-esteem in the control group before and after SDS intervention (high score: t=-0.35, p=0.7281; low score: t=-1.26, p=0.2161) (see Table 17). The experimental group showed higher self-esteem levels as tested by the mean differences between post- versus pre-evaluation scores on self-esteem at the 0.0001 level (high, 4.81 and low, -4.75) (see Table 17).

Table 18 shows the mean change results for self-esteem in the control versus experimental groups (t=-3.70, p=0.0005). No significant changes were noted for the low level of self-esteem (t=1.63, p=0.1094). These results suggest that even though the low self-esteem subscale did not change significantly, the PFC's level of high self-esteem increased in a positive direction for the experimental group after the SDS intervention was administered.

*Table 17. Self-Esteem Mean Differences Between Post- Versus Pre-
Evaluation of Primary Family Caregivers*

	Control Group (N=30)			Experimental Group (N=30)		
	Mean	t	p-value	Mean	t	p-value
Self-Esteem						
High	-1.7	-0.35	0.7281	2.4	4.81	0.0001
Low	-0.9	-1.26	0.2161	-2.3	-4.75	0.0001

*Table 18. Self-Esteem: T-Test Results of PTCs--Control Versus
Experimental Groups*

	Control Group (N=30)			Experimental Group (N=30)		
	Mean	t	p-value	Mean	t	p-value
Self-Esteem						
High	-1.7	-0.35	0.7281	2.4	4.81	0.0001
Low	-0.9	-1.26	0.2161	-2.3	-4.75	0.0001

In conclusion, the data presented on self-esteem in this study support Hypothesis 1: PFCs will report higher levels of self-esteem post-SDS intervention, and those levels will be higher than the PFCs in the control group.

Hypothesis 2

Hypothesis 2: There will be decreased levels of enmeshment following SDS intervention for the experimental subjects compared to subjects in the control group.

Family Cohesion and Adaptability

Scores on FACES II were computed for the experimental and control groups on the PFCs pre- and post-intervention. The two dimensions of caregivers' behavior that were evaluated were cohesion and adaptability so as to show the stability of the PFCs. The differences in the mean scores evaluating these caregiver variables were not statistically significant. Cohesion for the control group was 54.3 pre-intervention and 62.7 post-intervention, and 52.9 pre-intervention and 52.8 post-intervention for the experimental group (see Table 19).

Table 19. Cohesion and Adaptability Mean Scores and Standard Deviations for Evaluation of Status of Primary Family Caregivers

Variable	Control Group (N=30)		Experimental Group (N=30)	
	Pre	Post	Pre	Post
Cohesion	54.3	62.7	52.9	52.8
	(9.51)	(10.15)	(8.97)	(9.41)
Adaptability	46.6	50.1	46.1	47.3
	(8.40)	(7.93)	(9.73)	(9.73)
(Standard Deviation)				

The means for the post- versus pre-evaluation scores on cohesion for the control group were significantly different (X=8.4; t=3.87;

p=0.0006) from the experimental group's cohesion scores ($\overline{X}$=-0.0; t=-0.02; p=0.9830) (see Table 20).

Table 20. Mean Differences Between Post- Versus Pre-Evaluation Cohesion and Adaptation Scores of PFCs

	Control Group (N=30)			Experimental Group (N=30)		
	Mean	t	p-value	Mean	t	p-value
Cohesion	8.4	3.87	0.0006	-0.0	-0.02	0.9830
Adaptability	3.5	2.07	0.0537	1.2	0.80	0.4315

The scores on FACES II indicated that the control group's PFCs' family were more cohesive post-intervention than the experimental group's. Some factors that may have contributed to this were that the control group PFCs interacted in a positive manner with the care recipient; family loyalty was more interdependent than in the experimental group; and family members were less involved in each other's lives. However, when t-test results were assessed, there was a statistically significant change observed in the control versus experimental group after the intervention (t=3.16; p=0.0025. Thus, the results indicated that the intervention had a positive effect on the cohesion aspect of family functioning in the experimental group (see Table 21).

The adaptability dimension of FACES II showed no statistically significant change in the control versus the experimental group scores (control group: $\overline{X}$=46.6 pre-intervention, $\overline{X}$=50.1 post-intervention; experimental group $\overline{X}$=46.1 pre-intervention, $\overline{X}$=47.3 post-intervention) (see Table 19).

The adaptability mean score for FACES II between the post- versus pre-evaluation scores was not different statistically for the control ($\overline{X}$=3.5; t=2.01; p=0.0537) and experimental ($\overline{X}$=1.2; t=0.80;

p=0.4315) groups (see Table 20). T-test results for the adaptability dimension showed no significant difference in the control and experimental group scores (t=0.99; p=0.3260) (see Table 21). Olson (1989) classified a high cohesive and a high adaptability family as balanced. Therefore, the PFCs in both the experimental and control groups were similar at baseline.

Table 21. Cohesion and Adaptability T-Test Results of Control Versus Experimental Groups

	Control Mean	Experimental Mean	t-test	p-value
Cohesion	8.4	-0.0	3.16	0.0025
Adaptability	3.5	1.2	0.99	0.3260

To note whether the caregivers were enmeshed with the care recipient, the researcher used the global rating observational assessment of the Clinical Rating Scale (CRS) proposed by Olson (1993). "The global rating should be based on overall evaluation or gestalt rather than a sum of the sub-scale ratings. Then it becomes possible to classify the...family into one of the four levels of cohesion (disengaged, separated, connected or enmeshed) and one of four levels of family adaptability (rigid, structured, flexible and chaotic)" (p. 1). The interrater reliability of the clinical rating scale was derived from the Family Interaction Project. The reliability coefficiency for cohesion and adaptability was 0.95 and 0.94, respectively, and the CRS alpha reliability for cohesion was 0.95 and 0.94 for adaptability (Thomas & Olson, 1993).

In comparing the qualitative data globally between the control and experimental groups pre-intervention, enmeshment was high. Interpreting the results in the context of caregiving, the PFC was primarily an authoritarian, but when some democratic negotiations are needed, he/she is flexible enough to get things done. The family rules and roles can be shifted to accommodate the familial situation (adaptability dimension).

The enmeshed caregiver is overworked, inattentive to personal needs, frustrated, apathetic, depressed, socially isolated and lonely (Jed, 1989). This assessment of the PFC is further supported by the qualitative data. (Refer to the qualitative section of this study for a complete discussion.)

In conclusion, the data presented on enmeshment in this study supports Hypothesis 2: PFCs in the experimental group reported lower levels of enmeshment post-SDS intervention as compared to PFCs in the control group.

Hypothesis 3

Hypothesis 3: There will be increased use of health services utilization among experimental subjects compared to subjects in the control group following the SDS intervention. However, the results of this study showed that decreased enmeshment in the experimental PFCs did not result in an increased use of health service agencies as compared to the control group (see Table 13).

The control group PFCs used health service agencies such as nurse aide services, home maker chore, hospital care, social workers and church members more frequently than the experimental group members. Both groups primarily used family members as helpers to decrease the strain of caregiving before and after SDS intervention. African-Americans in this study used religion as a coping strategy to reduce burden and burnout. Chi-square results indicated that there was no association between the experimental and control groups' PFCs' use of religious dimensions such as religious articles, music, bible reading, private prayers, church attendance, and talking about religion with others (see Tables 22 and 23).

Table 22. Chi-Square Analysis of the Care Recipients' Dimensions of Religiosity (N=60)

Characteristic	Control Group (N=30)		Experimental Group (N=30)	
	No.	%	No.	%
Religious Articles (X^2=0.10; p-value=0.754^{NS})				
Present	24	80.00	23	76.67
Not Present	6	20.00	7	23.33
Religious Music (X^2=0.69; p-value=0.405^{NS})				
Present	8	26.67	11	36.67
Not Present	22	73.33	19	63.33
Bible Reading (X^2=0.48; p-value=0.924^{NS})				
Never	4	13.33	3	10.00
Sometimes Daily	18	60.00	18	60.00
Several Times A Day	7	23.33	7	23.33
Twice A Week	1	3.33	2	6.67

Table 23. Chi-Square Analysis of the Dimensions of Religiosity of PFCs (N=60)

Characteristic	Control Group (N=30)		Experimental Group (N=30)	
	No.	%	No.	%
Private Praying (X^2=0.10; p-value=0.628^{NS})				
Sometimes	8	12.67	5	16.67
Daily	9	30.00	11	36.67
Several Times A Day	13	43.33	14	46.67

Table 23 continued

Characteristic	Control Group (N=30)		Experimental Group (N=30)	
	No.	%	No.	%
Church Attendance (X^2=5.42; p-value=0.247[NS])				
Daily	1	3.33	2	6.67
Once A Week	15	50.00	8	26.67
Once A Month	7	23.33	6	20.00
Twice A Month	2	6.67	2	6.67
Never	5	16.67	12	40.00
Bible Reading (Self) (X^2=2.87; p-value=0.411[NS])				
Never	4	13.33	1	3.33
Sometimes	9	30.00	11	36.67
Daily	12	40.00	10	33.33
Several Times A Day	5	16.67	8	26.67
Rate of Congregational Activity (X^2=3.46; p-value=0.063[NS])				
Very Active	15	50.00	8	26.67
Inactive	15	50.00	22	73.33
Religious Talking With Others (X^2=0.80; p-value=0.849[NS])				
Never	4	13.33	3	10.00
Daily	12	40.00	10	33.33
Several Times A Day	1	3.33	2	6.67

Hypothesis 4

Hypothesis 4: There will be decreased caregiver burden and caregiver burnout in experimental subjects after SDS intervention compared to subjects in the control group (see Table 24).

Caregiver Burden

The burden score was computed as a total score from the responses of the PFC in both the control and experimental groups' pre- and post-intervention. For the control group, caregiver burden increased from a mean score of 40.9 to 45.3 post-intervention. The experimental group's burden mean score decreased significantly from 47.4 pre-intervention to a mean score of 23.2 post-intervention (see Table 24).

Table 24. Burden and Burnout Mean Scores for Evaluation of Primary Family Caregivers

Variable	Control Group (N=30)		Experimental Group (N=30)	
	Pre	Post	Pre	Post
Burden	40.9	45.3	47.4	23.2
	(21.32)	(15.80)	(18.72)	(13.18)
Burnout				
Emotional Exhaustion	35.6	38.3	40.1	15.0
	(14.07)	(15.44)	(11.66)	(11.68)
Depersonalization	5.6	4.7	5.7	0.5
	(6.37)	(5.22)	(6.03)	(1.33)
Personal	27.1	37.0	27.7	38.9
Accomplishment	(4.93)	(5.27)	(4.52)	(4.94)
(Standard Deviation)				

It is interesting to note that the mean differences between the control and experimental groups' post- versus pre-evaluation burden scores, as shown in Table 25, are statistically significant at p=0.0001 ($\bar{X}$=-24.2; t=-6.23) for the experimental group and the control group's burden score results are not statistically significant at a p-value of 0.1746 ($\overline{X}$=4.4; t=1.39). The t-test scores on burden of the PFCs in the control group versus experimental group were significant at p < 0.0001 with a t=5.71 (see Table 26). In terms of burden, the experimental PFCs' burden scores changed post-intervention more significantly in a positive direction than the scores in the control group.

Table 25. Burden and Burnout Mean Differences Between Post- Versus Pre-Evaluation Scores of PFCs

	Control Group (N=30)			Experimental Group (N=30)		
	Mean	t	p-value	Mean	t	p-value
Burden	4.4	1.39	0.1746	-24.2	-6.23	0.0001
Burnout						
Emotional Exhaustion	2.7	0.98	0.3369	-25.1	-10.73	0.0001
Depersonal- ization	-0.9	-0.68	0.5010	-5.2	-4.79	0.0001
Personal Accomplishment	9.9	7.36	0.0001	11.2	8.86	0.0001

Caregiver Burnout

A modified Maslach Burnout Inventory was used to evaluate PFC burnout. Mean scores and their post-/pre-intervention differences were computed for the three sections of the instrument: emotional exhaustion, depersonalization and personal accomplishment (see Tables 24, 25 and 26). Normative data on African-American PFCs of frail homebound elderly have not been established on all the subscales of the burnout inventory, although Maslach and Jackson (1981) did study a racially mixed sample of professional caregivers, but not African-American family caregivers.

Table 26. Burden and Burnout T-Test Results of Control Versus Experimental Groups

	Control	Experimental	t-test	p-value
Burden	4.1	-24.2	5.71	<0.0001
Burnout Emotional Exhaustion	2.7	-25.1	7.63	<0.0001
Depersonal- ization	-0.9	-5.2	2.59	0.0120
Personal Accomplishment	9.9	11.3	-0.76	0.4519

The differences in mean burnout scores in the control and experimental groups were statistically significant on all three subscales of burnout: emotional exhaustion, depersonalization and personal accomplishment, with a p-value of 0.0001 (see Table 26). T-test evaluation of mean differences were not statistically significant for the control group on the emotional exhaustion subscale. The data showed that personal accomplishment increased in the experimental group (t=8.86; p=0.0001). The control group's personal accomplishment dimension was statistically significant pre-SDS intervention. This result may indicate the PFCs were a relatively stable group of research participants. They were satisfied with their choice of caregiving status. The mean change on this subscale was not significantly different from pre- to post-test (see Table 26) which can be interpreted as the PFCs being equally satisfied with their accomplishments in their caregiving duties over the course of the study. African-American PFCs take pride in their caregiving: caring for a frail relative in the home was a family expectation. They also take pride in their love, religion, obligations and choice of caregiving help in tasks and personal accomplishments, as supported by the qualitative data in this chapter.

The data support Hypothesis 4, in that burden and burnout decreased following the SDS intervention on the experimental group subjects. The Maslach Burnout Inventory was reliable in the dimensions of emotional exhaustion and depersonalization. On the personal accomplishment subscale, Cronbach's alpha was extremely low pre-intervention (.17), as well as low post-intervention (.48). These findings suggest instability of the instrument in measuring African-American PFCs' sense of personal accomplishment as a component of burnout. Instead, the results may reflect PFCs' pride in caregiving; that is, not wanting to be seen as "failures" by other family members and/or outsiders. It is possible that the PFCs may have misinterpreted the Maslach Burnout Inventory personal accomplishment subscale items, as is reflected in the following statements:

> "I can easily understand how my relative feels about things."

> "I deal very effectively with the problems of my relative."

> "I feel happy after working closely with my relative."

> "I have done many worthwhile things in my caregiving job."

Therefore, this subscale needs to be replicated among African-American PFCs.

Research Question

This research was undertaken to answer the following question: What is the effect of the SDS intervention on self-esteem, health services utilization, enmeshment, burden, and burnout on African-American family caregivers of homebound frail elderly? Figure 11 shows the effect the SDS intervention had on self-esteem (increased), health service utilization (no change), and enmeshment, burden and burnout (decreased) of African-American family caregivers of homebound frail elderly.

QUALITATIVE ANALYSIS

The data reported in this section came from the family information collected during the third through tenth sessions of the experimental PFCs' interviews. Rew, Bechtel and Sapp (1993) stated that "qualitative nursing research is a systematic method of inquiry that enables the researcher to answer important questions about phenomena of concern to nursing" (p. 300). The purpose of the qualitative component was to provide additional data to answer the research question "What is the effect of the SDS intervention on self-esteem, service utilization, enmeshment, burden and burnout on African-American family caregivers of homebound frail elderly?," and to complement and enhance the quantitative data.

The researcher used the Satir paradigm (see Figure 2) for change as a means of gathering data on intergenerational family pattern for caregiving, rebuilding self-esteem, decreasing enmeshment, burden, and burnout, and increasing health services utilization of the PFC. The SDS nursing intervention model was the focus of the context during the interviews in order to help the PFC become more aware of how his/her caregiving tasks affected him/her.

Satir and her colleagues (1991) viewed the essence of change as a means for helping people to grow. Creating intentional change involves processing the unknown. The PFCs' communication pattern(s), family rules, methods of dealing with anger, and self-esteem issues were explored in relation to Satir's change process (see Figure 12).

The Satir change process consists of six stages: (1) status quo--an indication that a change in the system is needed; (2) foreign element--a desire for change that is articulated by someone in the system; (3) chaos--anxiety that moves the system toward risk-taking behaviors; (4) integrating new behaviors--a conscious period in which the person chooses comfort over familiarity; (5) practicing new behaviors--a conscious effort to practice, confirm, validate and reconnect new

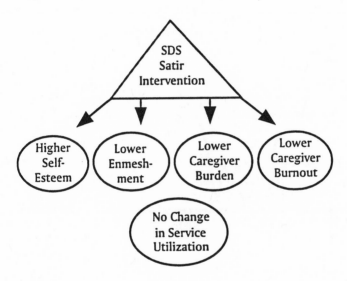

Figure 11. Diagram of Caregiver Burnout After SDS Intervention

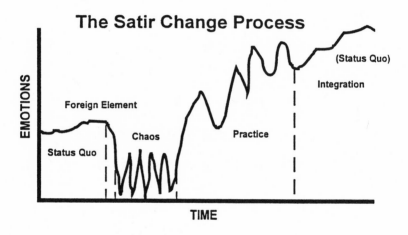

Figure 12. The Satir Change Process

behaviors to the self and others; and (6) new status quo--the person is open to new possibilities and information.

Dodson (1991) states that Satir viewed change as an ongoing unconscious process which, when taken in a one-to-one context, such as caregiving, the cathartic experience is one of letting go of past feelings. The PFCs in the experimental group demonstrated change during the interview process. (See the following field note examples for experimental group (PFCs) only.) The researcher used field notes to provide a context for analyzing each PFC's level of self-esteem, enmeshment, burden, burnout and rate of health services utilization.

Self-Esteem

Self-esteem, as defined by Satir and her colleagues (1991), is being in tune to all levels of one's personhood. During the third through seventh interview sessions, the PFCs showed evidence of low self-esteem by giving statements such as:

"I just sit and look when something is wrong."

"I am really a placator. I don't cross my husband."

"My mother felt sorry for herself and I feel sorry for myself."

"I was sensitive and afraid of my father."

"I feel inadequate and unable to defend myself. I stay quiet when people are upset with me."

"I was the type of person who gave everything to everybody. I am still doing it."

"I protect my feelings."

"I don't care about myself. I just want to be human."

"My motto in life is: blessings don't come from the one you help."

These statements illustrate themes of low self-worth patterns such as "I am not loved," "I am dependent," "I fear change," and "I am rigid and I need to be a placator, a blamer, irrelevant or superreasonable to survive."

The PFCs began to feel more positive about themselves as the SDS intervention progressed. (These interview sessions were the eighth, ninth, tenth and twelfth sessions.) They made statements such as:

> "I am content with my life...I have made arrangements with my sister that if something happens to me that she would take care of my husband. I don't want him to go into a nursing home. She has agreed. I will care for her if she needs it. The last person will get an outsider to help and our property will belong to him."

> "I can see a change every day of my life and in my caregiving. I have the ability to do what I have to do."

> "It's hard at times caring for her and seeing her health fail her, but this caring I have for her is unspeakable joy. She in her own way loves me."

> "Now I have choices. I am aware of what I say to others and how I say it. I won't get trapped again. I am much happier. I know that my self-esteem has improved since you have been talking with me."

> "I have been unleashed. I don't know what I have become, but I know I am different. I feel good about the way I communicate with my family now."

> "I had it hard. My brothers and sisters were all separated and brought up by different aunts and uncles. So taking care of my aunt is my good deed to her."

> "I feel good about my caregiving. But there is always room for improvement."

"I am not depressed. I used to hold everything in...I cried all the time. Now I am free as a butterfly."

"I feel I have gained the power not to be afraid."

"I like being a caregiver. I like dealing with elderly people. My caregiving extends beyond my family."

"In my family, we know each other's habits. I usually express myself and get things off my chest."

"I feel good about me. I feel I do real good in my caregiving."

"I take one day at a time. I thank God for my day every day."

These statements suggest that over the course of the study, the PFCs began to be more open and flexible. They became choice makers who were more aware of how they participated in their caregiving roles and welcomed change, thereby increasing their self-esteem.

Enmeshment

Enmeshment is emotional closeness in family relations where family members maintain the status quo and submerge issues of conflict (Satir, et al., 1991). The following quotes (taken from interview sessions three through eight) illustrate enmeshment as part of the PFCs' coping pattern while carrying out their caregiving tasks:

"When I leave my husband with others, I constantly worry about him until I return. I rush back because I worry about things here."

"When I can't take Mama with me, I worry until I get back home."

"I am doing what my mom wants me to do."

"My family is very close, one cannot fall without the other. But they have their families to care for also."

"I am very close to my mother. My family will come and help me with my mother, but I don't ask them."

"I have always felt bound to care for my parents, as if it was my mission in life."

"I had no other choice but to become my mother's caregiver. I never left home. My family is very close."

"In my family when one of us has a problem, we all have a problem."

"I have nothing to do except take care of my wife. She is all I have. If she doesn't sleep, I don't sleep."

"If I go to church or leave the house, I am tense and worried about how she is doing."

"My mother only calls me when she needs something and that's all the time. I get a break when she is sleeping. She remembers no one but my name."

"My husband is my responsibility. I don't keep anything hidden from him."

"My husband is boss of the house. My motto for life is: try to live the best I can for the Lord and my father. No burden, just loneliness."

"Caregiving is like a family affair. It's like we read each other's mind."

High enmeshment was evident in the PFCs' relationship with their family. There were diffused boundaries, overinvolvement, and increased family loyalty, thereby a feeling of being closed to outsiders, change and self-growth. The change process (first level change) that developed over the course of the intervention was evident in the PFCs' movement toward family autonomy, flexibility, interdependence in family loyalty, open communication with outsiders and an openness to change. The following statements, taken from sessions nine and twelve, illustrate the experimental group PFCs' de-enmeshment patterns:

> "My family shares everything. We laugh, we cry, and we sing together. We take care of each other."

> "I am not burdened. How can I burn out? I love doing this. My daddy would always say, 'get up in the morning, if you have nothing to do at all.'"

> "This is not like the end of the world. You make adjustments. My family works together. We are very close."

> "My family helps with money. We are close. They come when I need them to help with Mama."

> "My family is very close. I don't make a habit out of using my family members to help me. If I need help, my nieces will come by and help me out."

> "My family is my backup system. My husband does as much for himself as he can. I have help and I only do when I have to."

> "My family is very close knit. I am happy doing what I want to do."

Burden

According to Satir and her colleagues (1991), burden is a loss of hope and feeling overwhelmed by care responsibilities and daily hassles. Inflexibility, familial tension, and increased financial strain are examples of burden frequently reported by caregivers. The PFCs acknowledged being burdened while caring for the care recipient pre-intervention. The following quotations reflect caregiver burden:

"I am my husband's only help."

"I have no stop sign in my life; therefore, I don't fail."

"I suffer with hypertension, lower left leg pain, and headaches. Caregiving has taken its toll on me."

"At night, I go back and forth checking on her...she is the boss."

"I am still scorching, but have not burnt out yet."

"I am getting tired, but my aunt has no one to care for her. She does not have enough money to be placed in the nursing home. I will have to quit my job to take care of her...her health is going down."

"I take pride in what I can do, but I can't continue to take care of others. My health is failing me."

"I get frustrated in my caregiving."

"I have no help with my wife. My son lives away. He comes in on the holidays and does things but it's not like having him home with us."

"I can't make plans for me. This keep me on the edge. I am overworked."

"I have lived a life. I must take care of my husband. I am afraid to go to the store. I feel the need to be here for him."

"Yes, I am burdened. I have high blood pressure, stress and depression."

"Sometimes he doesn't want me to leave. Staying all the time wears me out."

"I am financially burdened, but I will not put my Mama in a nursing home to work. I made this choice. It takes talent to make ends meet in this household every month, but we manage."

"I keep busy. I don't sit down and take it easy. I can't. I have to be here for my mama."

"I am proud of my family. We are very close, but I don't depend on no one but myself."

"I am grateful that my wife does not have a breakdown. I don't know if I can take that."

"I am burdened sometimes. Burnout comes when you don't have someone to help you and you have no way out."

"My husband is dependent on me. I don't know what else to do."

Descriptions of caregiver burden were prevalent in the PFC's life. Decreased burden and reliance on religion were also evident during the intervention phase of this study.

In terms of coping with burden, religion was a strategy used by both African-American PFCs and their care recipients. Dimensions of religiosity in both the PFC and care recipients were assessed by observation and asking what role religion played in the PFC's life. Chi-square results showed that both the control and experimental groups were not statistically different on dimensions of religiosity.

Percentage response rates for the control group (N=30) and the experimental group (N=30) on the religiosity dimension were as follows: presence of religious articles in care recipient's bedroom: 80% control, 77% experimental (X^2=0.098; df=1; p=0.754); presence of religious music in care recipient's bedroom: 27% control, 37% experimental (X^2=0.693; df=1; p=0.405); and, sometimes Bible reading to the care recipient: 60% for both control and experimental group (X^2=0.476; df=3; p=0.924). These results illustrated that religion was a vital source of support to the care recipient as performed by the PFC (see Table 22).

The PFCs are not only advocates providing informal religious support to the care recipient, but they also support their own spiritual involvement and emotional well-being. The data presented in Table 23 show the percentage response rates of PFCs and religious variable dimensions for both the control and experimental groups. The dimensions that were used "daily" and "sometimes daily" were private praying, church attendance, Bible reading and talking about religion with others. The PFCs tended not to be active in congregational activities, but these religious dimensions provided spiritual support to them. Religion as a support network that contributes to the feeling of well-being in both African-American PFCs and their care recipients was evident in this study. Several studies in the literature also support that religion has a beneficial effect on African-American elderly (Chatters, Taylor & Jackson, 1986; Krause, 1992; Taylor & Chatters, 1986a; Walls, 1992). Thus, it appears that a high percentage of the PFCs used religion as a supportive role in decreasing enmeshment, burden and the potential for burnout in family caregiving role. Since religion contributes to spiritual well-being of the PFCs and their care recipients, it is logical to assume that caregiver burden will be decreased through use of this coping mechanism.

Decreased burden and reliance on religion are also prevalent in the following statements taken from family interview data:

> "I have everything I need. That's all God promised."

> "We are rope holders for one another; therefore, we must have faith in one another."

> "I depend on the Lord."

> "Through my caregiving, I have Jesus."

> "I have worked all my life. Now that I am 66 years old, I am still trying to make it. I must be content with my caregiving."

> "One thing I know, God is using me."

> "I believe in the Serenity Prayer."

"I am burdened, but I cast them to the Lord and He gives me strength."

"Structure is what I need...rest, eat, drink and clean."

"I push caregiving aside sometimes. I read a lot."

"This does not bother me. Everybody has something in his life to face."

"I am burdened sometimes but my daughters come to the rescue. My family is very close. I don't think I will ever burnout."

"God don't put no more on you than we could bear."

"My family help each other."

Decreased caregiver burden, as an aspect of the SDS intervention model, facilitated openness in communication, flexibility, increased energy, and diminished familial tension, thus promoting improved ability to resolve overwhelming daily caregiver hassles.

Burnout

Burnout in the caregiving context is what Satir calls responding to overload in caregiving tasks. These data are illustrated by PFC statements pre-intervention as follows:

"I suffer from migraine headaches and I am overweight."

"I must stay on my routine; I don't deviate. I can't poke around. I must do what I have to do and get it over with."

"Burnout is a problem. Sometimes I feel like giving up but who in my family would carry the load. There is nobody. My children are not like me."

"I feel tired, frustrated and lonely."

"I get depressed, to the point that I have a migraine headache for days."

"I am content while I am at home, but if I go out and leave him with someone, I am tense and I hurry to get back home. This really tires me out."

"I am tired. Burnout is nothing. I will never get tired of taking care of my mother."

"Organization and structure are what I enjoy doing because this really works for me. I don't like problems."

"It is hard for me to care for my mother; sometimes I don't care."

"I became ill...I was about to give in but my mother wanted to come and live with me. I do what I have to do."

"In my mind, I ask, why me? I am cut off from things. I am at home all the time."

"I feel like a slave. I have this to do."

High caregiver burnout has been associated with dullness, malaise, rigidity, irritability, depression, crankiness, reactive communication and an inability to communicate effectively in an assertive manner (Goldstein, 1979; Jed, 1989; Lindgren, 1990; Morris, Morris & Britton, 1988). Over the course of the interviews, some of the PFCs using the SDS intervention model demonstrated a decrease in caregiver burnout by becoming proactive decision makers, more charismatic, energetic and less depressed. The following statements show evidence of decreased burnout:

"I don't hold nobody in my heart."

"I am a caregiver from my heart. I would not burn
out because I have some nursing training. I know how
to take care of the sick and myself."

"I structure my day. No burnout here. I experiment
with myself to do well."

"I help myself...I don't overexert myself. Do for
yourself 'cause no one will do for you."

"I don't worry, I pray. God has a lot of surprises for
us."

Health Services Utilization

There were only two statements given by the PFCs regarding the
use of any formal assistance in their caregiving tasks. These were:
"I am my husband's only help," and "I really enjoy my wife being at
home. I asked the doctor to discharge her from the nursing home so I
could take care of her at home." As noted in the quantitative data (see
Table 13), the PFCs did not use health care agencies pre- or post-
intervention as their resources of choice because family members (83%)
in both the control and experimental groups provided the main support
system.

Summary of Qualitative Data

In summary, the results of the intervention protocol (see Figure 13)
using the Satir change process indicated there was generational
patterning of family caregiving among the PFCs in the experimental
group. PFCs appreciated and let go of their past as much as possible so
as to re-experience feelings in a safe and accepting environment. The
PFCs became validated as persons of worth. They acknowledged new
possibilities in caregiving, and they were willing to take new risks in
the interest of the self. Satir calls this internal shift "first level change.
"First level change is when one becomes aware, acknowledges, owns,
manages and enjoys one's feelings (Satir, et al., 1991).

SUMMARY OF FINDINGS

In this chapter, the results of the study were presented relative to the hypotheses and the research question. The main findings of this study were that the PFCs and care recipients in both the control and experimental groups were primarily females between the ages of 60 to 79. The reasons for the care recipient being homebound were both physical illness and disorientation. Generally, care recipients in both groups did not change in their mental status and activities of daily living before and after the SDS nursing intervention model.

The PFCs' self-esteem, enmeshment, burden and burnout scores changed as a result of the SDS nursing intervention model. Thus, Hypotheses 1, 2 and 4 were supported by these data for the experimental group PFCs. Hypothesis 3 was not supported by the data. The caregivers continued to assume total responsibility for the care recipient. The most frequently used category of health services utilization were family members, and the evidence showed there was little or no use of formal health care agencies pre- and post-intervention.

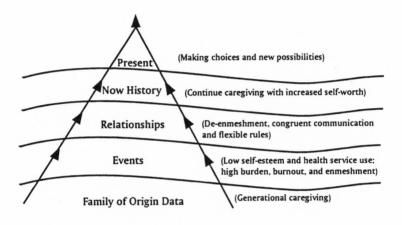

Figure 13. Intervention Protocol: First Level Change Process--
Awareness and Acceptance

V

Discussion and Implications

In this chapter, findings will be discussed relative to a nursing intervention model, SDS, that used the Satir family tools. The purposes, methodology and findings of the study will provide the foundations and recommendations for further study.

The purposes of the study were to test a nursing intervention model, Self-Directed Skills (SDS), by determining the effectiveness of the model on the PFC who provides 60-75 percent of the care of an African-American homebound frail elderly relative. The study specifically aimed to: (1) implement and evaluate the SDS nursing intervention model using the Satir paradigm, and (2) evaluate the differences between the experimental and control groups on levels of self-esteem, enmeshment, service utilization, burden and burnout.

Sixty African-American PFCs and their elderly care recipients were interviewed by the researcher after being randomly assigned either to a control group or an experimental group. The researcher evaluated the care recipient's mental status (35 females and 25 males) using Kahn's Mental Status Questionnaire and their functional level of performance using Katz's Activities of Daily Living Index. The PFCs (46 females and 14 males) completed Rosenberg's Self-Esteem Scale, Zarit's Burden Scale, a modified Maslach Burnout Inventory, Olson's Family Adaptability and Cohesion Evaluation Scale II, and a checklist of what health service agencies they used.

Three research assistants were assigned to do friendly visits with the control group. The researcher carried out the intervention protocol, the experiential teaching-learning cycle, and the Satir change process (see Figures 2 and 8) for the experimental group. Both groups received 24 contact hours. Demographic findings revealed that the PFCs in both groups were similar. The care recipients in experimental and control groups were also similar at baseline.

A discussion of the findings and nursing implications will be presented in the context of the predictive statement before and after the SDS nursing intervention model (see Figure 1) and the results of the quantitative and qualitative data. Recommendations for further study and for nursing practice will also be discussed.

DISCUSSION OF FINDINGS

Essentially this study tested an intervention model using the Satir family tools (SDS model). Comparison of the experimental and control group results showed differences in the pre-/post-SDS nursing intervention model. In the experimental group, post-SDS intervention findings revealed that the PFCs' scores for caregiver burden and caregiver burnout were reduced and their self-esteem scores were increased. Enmeshment global rating results showed differences in the control and experimental group status pre- and post-intervention.

With regard to self-esteem, the paired t-test results showed that PFCs' self-esteem in the experimental group increased (see Table 19) when the researcher made contact with the PFC and the care recipient and explored self-growth in the context of family caregiving. Qualitative data statements made by the PFCs at the beginning of the sessions revealed their experience of low self-esteem: "I don't feel good about myself." However, qualitative statements made by PFC's during later sessions of the encounters expressed higher self-esteem; for example: "I have developed new ways of seeing myself. I have new possibilities."

The use of FACES II as a measure for enmeshment in the PFCs proved to be a problem. The instrument was not sensitive in testing mean change in this population (using the cohesion and adaptability subscale findings). The use of the Clinical Rating Scale, as recommended by Olson (1991), supported that PFCs were enmeshed.

Caregiver burden and burnout decreased in PFCs following implementation of the SDS nursing intervention model. Health services utilization showed no change from pre- to post-intervention over the course of the study for either group.

The research findings supported several of Satir's assumptions regarding family and individual integrity; that people are unique; internal change is possible; we all have the internal resources we need in order to cope successfully and to grow; people learn survival/coping in their family of origin; and, congruence and high self-esteem are major goals in the SDS nursing intervention model. Therefore, it appears that appreciating and accepting the past increases the ability of PFCs to manage their present. The past does not have to contaminate the present. The two variables (self-esteem and enmeshment) used in the Satir paradigm are seen as learned behaviors. The behaviors can be altered/changed through the use of the Satir change process. The Satir change process is based on family of origin information between the primary triad--mother, father and child. The parents teach the child how to deal with inner conflicts and the world. This learning can or cannot be validated at times by the individual. Satir uses the primary triad to emphasize the essential source of identity of the self (Satir, et al, 1991). Therefore, PFCs' family data (the primary triad) may be used to explore, modify and change their perceptions of caregiving.

Dysfunctional learning also comes from the primary triad. The individual yearns for completeness, but past events cause him/her to have low self-esteem and high enmeshment. To facilitate high self-esteem and low enmeshment (which is the goal of the Satir change process), the SDS nursing intervention conveys the incongruent information and provides the PFC with an experience in the present, thus causing a transformation process to take place.

The Satir model looks at the family as a three generational system. The intervention is based on growth and not pathology. The nurse researcher using this model can add to the person's self-growth and harness more positive behaviors. To be able to do this, the nurse researcher must understand and be grounded in the Satir model, be aware of his/her own limitations, and must have formal training in the Satir model.

The goal of the Satir model used in this study was to help the PFC develop into an independent family member who has the skills to cope and make decisions that work for him or her. The ability of the PFC to promote self-growth, make choices and become aware of his or her own needs was the overall purpose of the conceptual model used (Satir & Baldwin, 1983). Taken together, the pattern of family caregiving for a frail relative at home and the total responsibilities for this care recipient can be viewed as an emotional cost to the PFC (Lindgren, 1990; Zarit, et al., 1980). Comparing the results of the data from the experimental and control groups showed that the SDS nursing intervention was an effective model in reducing the emotional cost of caregiving.

Recruitment of research participants was a challenge due to the selection criteria being restricted to care recipients with frail health status, the expectation of African-American church leaders who lived in the South, and the time commitment of the PFCs to the study (24 hours divided into three 2-hour sessions per week for four weeks). To obtain a sample size of 60 PFCs and care recipients, the researcher interviewed 105 potential subjects. Therefore, generalizability of the results to African-American PFCs and care recipients must be done with caution.

Figure 1 illustrates the predictive and hypothesized outcomes of the variables studied. The findings indicate that using the Satir SDS intervention was effective in increasing self-esteem and decreasing burden and burnout. Formal health services utilization remained low among the study sample. Enmeshment differences were noted pre- and post-intervention as defined by Satir. Olson's FACES II instrument measured cohesion and adaptability of the PFC which were used as pre-intervention status assessment of the PFCs (Fettler, 1994). The family remained the support agent for caregiving among this sample of African-American PFCs because the SDS model only produced first level change (Satir, 1991), in which the PFCs are aware of caregiving options. It could be argued that they made objective choices not to use formal health care agencies. This may have been related to the researcher being grounded in the Satir Model; therefore, the PFCs were empowered internally so as to have less need for use of formal health care agencies. Rather, they are committed to family relationships for emotional, financial, physical, spiritual, psychological and social support. Results of this study support other research indicating that the family is the primary support agency for family caregivers of African-Americans (Chatters, et al., 1986; Gibson, 1989; Hinrichsen, et al., 1992; Jackson, 1970).

NURSING IMPLICATIONS

Implications from this study are focused on nursing practice, theory, education, and research. The research was designed to increase self-directed skills of PFCs who care for frail homebound elderly. Discussion of the SDS intervention used is warranted.

The findings indicated that the coping patterns of African-American PFCs of frail elderly in the home are costly, both physically and emotionally. Further research is necessary to determine whether the findings generated by this study are valid for other groups of PFCs and care recipients. The SDS nursing intervention model is a potentially effective tool for decreasing enmeshment, burden and burnout, and increasing self-esteem, but is ineffective in changing the PFCs' use of health service agencies (see Figure 10).

Because familial caregiving is an important concept in gerontology and supportive care for PFCs is stressed in the gerontological literature, intervention studies are needed to reduce enmeshment and caregiver burden and burnout and increase self-esteem. Community health nurses are in an ideal position to help PFCs and their care recipients determine what helps reduce enmeshment, burden and burnout and increase self-esteem and health services utilization. The use of health care agencies to reduce the potential for caregiver burden and burnout needs further study. For example, what is the impact of health care agencies on frail community elderly when Medicare days are used for home visits in relation to the reduction of caregiver burden and burnout?

NURSING PRACTICE

The researcher suggests that changes in PFCs be evaluated at six-month intervals so as to capture self-growth over time. Because of the increased number of PFCs in the African-American community caring for frail elderly, health care policies and outcome measures need to be designed to support and help pay the PFCs for home care. There is a need for home health nurses to be sensitive to PFCs' spiritual dimension of care so as to promote and enhance the religious qualities of African-American PFCs in the community. Additionally, home health nurses can formulate nursing interventions incorporating the use of prayer, religious songs (music), talking with others regarding religion, and using scripture-references in the plan of care for this population.

In the African-American community, there is a need for the PFCs to have a formal listing of health care agencies, purposes and costs so as to increase their use of these health care agencies. Community case managers can play a more central role in counseling and coordinating home care needs of care recipients so as to minimize the effects of caregiver burden and burnout. PFCs may need more one-to-one contact with other PFCs; therefore, support groups are suggested options for increasing social interactions, using churches attended by African-Americans for this purpose.

NURSING THEORY AND EDUCATION

Subjects in the experimental group participated in the Satir experiential teaching-learning process to improve self-care management skills. Rebuilding self-esteem of the PFCs, decreasing enmeshment, decreasing caregiver burden and burnout, and incorporating health care agencies into the care of the frail elderly is a feasible and important nursing outcome. The Satir model is teachable to family therapists and nurses in both undergraduate and graduate programs, and can facilitate specific therapeutic behaviors in nurses. Nurses who are educated in the Satir paradigm are then able to facilitate positive changes in PFCs. Therefore, it is recommended that schools of nursing increase family nursing content in the curriculum and emphasize the Satir model as a conceptual model that is taught as part of that curriculum.

Nursing theory development using the Satir model could promote family health care. The basic components of the model would include family data (family of origin, maternal and paternal maps), family rules, communication patterns, familial influences, and the Satir change process. (See Chapter II--Theoretical Framework: Satir Model for complete derivation of the projected theory model.)

The Satir model is process oriented and the foundation of the model is to increase self-directed skills of the client, including the self, the context, and the other (see Figure 2). Family nurse therapists must be theoretically grounded in the Satir model and trained in the Satir model, so as to properly implement interventions using the Satir family data tools.

NURSING RESEARCH

Review of the literature disclosed that there is a need to test the effects of caregiving on African-American PFCs. A study of this magnitude can be overwhelming, time consuming and costly. Yet, the study of African-American PFCs' coping patterns using conceptual models, such as Satir's model, is overdue. As the Satir model is utilized in practice, education and research, refinement of the model will occur, a nursing model will emerge, and nursing interventions will be implemented for PFCs who care for frail elderly in the community. Findings of this study indicated that a self-directed skills approach can decrease enmeshment and caregiver burden and burnout and increase self-esteem. Health services utilization results showed no change in PFCs' use of formal agencies.

In conclusion, the use of the Satir model had an effect on the African-American PFCs over the course of the study by increasing self-esteem and decreasing enmeshment and caregiver burden and burnout, but had no effect on health service utilization. However, there is a need for related investigations of importance to nursing practice, theory and education, and research. For example, data analysis could be done to address many unanswered questions, such as:

1. What role does religiosity play as a coping strategy for African-American PFCs in reducing caregiver burden and burnout?
2. What effects do friendly visits alone have on decreasing enmeshment and increasing self-esteem?
3. Why wasn't the personal accomplishment subscale on the Maslach Burnout Inventory sensitive enough to note caregiver burnout differences between the control and experimental PFCs pre and post intervention?
4. What do adaptability, cohesion and enmeshment mean in relation to the Satir/Olson models? [A triangulation procedure could be used to explore commonalities and differences in the two models.]
5. What effects did the researcher's personality and clinical expertise have on the PFCs' self-growth? [To test this research question, the research design would be similar but would use several researchers/clinicians grounded in the Satir paradigm. The same variables used in this study could be measured at different time intervals (e.g., sixth, ninth and twelfth sessions). This type of study would focus on comparing the PFC's self-esteem, enmeshment, caregiver burden and burnout, and health service utilization over time.

STUDY LIMITATIONS

Limitations of the study included the small sample size in one region of the country, making generalizability of the results limited only to the population studied. Also, recruitment of the study subjects was a challenge. The public service announcements were not an effective way of securing research participants due to a misunderstanding of the announcements and ministers wanting the researcher to start up mission groups for their sick and shut-in members, or wanting the researcher to service sick members of the church. The researcher collected data from all research participants and was not blinded to the treatment condition. Therefore, this could have indicated investigator bias.

Time constraints also limited the study in that the participants set the time frame for the research visit. After agreeing to the 24 hours of interview time, there were certain times of the day when the researcher could not visit the care recipient and PFC. Additionally, economic constraints also limited the study in that research assistants had to be hired to do friendly visits with the control group (24 hours each) (see Chapter III--Procedure for Control Group). The researcher had additional training in the Satir model (12 semester hours from the Satir Avanta Network). However, the self-growth and confidence shown by the PFCs in the experimental group subjects far outweighed the limitations cited in this section of the chapter.

The use of FACES II as an instrument for measuring enmeshment was problematic in this study and the results were not easily quantifiable. Instead, the researcher used Olson's Clinical Rating Scale and Satir's concept of enmeshment to interpret the qualitative findings from the PFCs' interviews. These findings suggest that the differences between the control and experimental group may be due to the FACES II instrument not measuring enmeshment specifically in relation to family cohesion and adaptability. Enmeshment was not measured several times over the course of the study. Further study of the effects associated with the enmeshment dimension is clearly in order, as well as a further examination of the SDS nursing intervention model in relation to caregiver enmeshment.

RECOMMENDATIONS FOR FURTHER STUDY

The SDS nursing intervention model tested in this study was an effective means of helping PFCs cope. Further research based on these findings might include the PFC participating in a Satir change process group over a four-week period (two-hour sessions); community health nurses counseling PFCs directly about self-esteem and familial caregiving responsibilities; and nurses providing information and opportunities for PFCs to increase their use of formal health service agencies so as to reduce some of their caregiving responsibilities and thus decrease burnout. The formal use of health service agencies by

African-American PFCs may be increased if the services become more culturally sensitive, are based in community churches, and are user friendly. Outcome measures need to be developed and tested for community health and geriatric nursing, and health care policy standards must be written for family home care of African-American PFCs. A research study comparing the Satir model variables to common caregiver variables found in the literature (e.g., depression, guilt, physical health and financial resources) would also be interesting.

In addition, future research efforts could explore data collectors' who are "blind" to treatment conditions of subjects to diminish change for investigator bias. It would also be interesting to follow up the qualitative data generated in this study in the future; e.g., have the PFCs in the experimental group describe a situation in which they have used the Satir change process while providing care.

Also, a comparison study of African-American and white PFCs using the Satir model needs to be conducted. It is impossible to compare the results of this study with results of previous studies on African-American caregivers, so this study needs to be replicated.

Future studies should also focus on identifying coping patterns of caregiving and family dynamics among PFCs and care recipients in relation to elder abuse, through evaluation of verbal and non-verbal communication interactions. Also, significant information can be gained by developing more culturally sensitive instruments related to coping patterns. Additionally, it would be interesting to systematically evaluate the coping benefits religion has in the daily life of the PFC. Tool development to measure religiosity in African-Americans is also needed.

SUMMARY OF FINDINGS

The purposes of this study were to test a nursing intervention model, Self-Directed Skills (SDS), to determine the effectiveness of the model on the PFC who provides 60 to 75 percent of the care of an African-American homebound frail elderly relative. The study specifically aimed to: (1) implement and evaluate the SDS nursing intervention model using the Satir paradigm and (2) evaluate the differences between the experimental and control groups on levels of self-esteem, enmeshment, service utilization, burden and burnout.

A sample of 60 PFCs and their care recipients participated in the study. The researcher utilized paired t-test and chi-square to statistically measure the mean differences between the control and experimental groups pre- and post-intervention model. Qualitative exemplars in verbatim format were presented to demonstrate low to high coping patterns of PFCs in the experimental group.

The findings of this study showed that the PFC pre-intervention had low self-esteem, burden and enmeshment; had a tendency for potential caregiver burnout; and did not use formal health care agencies. The SDS nursing intervention was effective for this sample because there were significant changes in the experimental group PFCs' self-esteem, burden, burnout and enmeshment, but not health services utilization.

Although this study demonstrated some interesting preliminary findings, it was carried out in a small sample of African-American Protestant sick and shut-in care recipients who had relatives who were the PFCs. Further, the experimental group was limited to the researcher's one-to-one contact for a one month period, while the control group was limited to one-to-one contact with the research assistants. The study should be replicated using a larger sample of PFCs in a caregiver support group setting using the Satir paradigm as the nursing intervention model.

Appendix

Satir Family Tools

The Self-Directed Skills (SDS) model was a systematic approach for processing the family dynamics of the PFCs. The following Satir family tools were used: family maps (family of origin, maternal and paternal), family rules, communication stances, the wheel of influence, the personal iceberg, the self-esteem maintenance kit, the self-mandala, and the change process.

Because the Satir family intervention tools were process oriented, the researcher used making contact, map reading, metaphors, sculpting, tracking, weaving, reframing, and the process of anchoring the new learning as a feedback mechanism for noting transformation in the PFC's caregiving behaviors. (See the following instructions for the Satir family tools.)

INSTRUCTIONAL SHEET FOR THE
SATIR INSTRUMENT PACKET

The investigator will form a one-to-one relationship with the caregiver and the care recipient. The family data packet will be completed by the investigator using the caregiver's responses during the interview process.

THE FAMILY MAP

The family map consists of your family's origin data (your father, mother and siblings). Note the family member's name, date of birth, place of birth, current age and/or the age at time of death, ethnic and religious background, occupation, education, health history and three descriptive adjectives that can be used to describe the family member. During your interaction with the investigator, you will share your feelings, family rules, family secrets and any significant health history about members of your family.

Procedures

The diagrams of your family of origin (maternal, paternal and current family) are to be done as outlined below:

Step I: Family of Origin

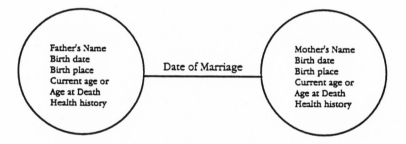

To this list, you might add: religious affiliation, occupation, ethnic background, education and hobbies.

Step II: Add three adjectives for each and identify the primary and secondary coping stances used by the parents when under stress.

Step III: Add the children as shown below. Add the same information for each child, as in Steps I and II. The lines denote strong, negative.

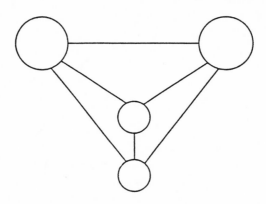

Step IV:

1. Do the same as Step III for maternal grandparents.
2. Do the same as Step III for paternal grandparents.
3. Do the same as Step III for current family.

Step V:

1. Give each of the three families a descriptive name.
2. Describe the significant symbols and rituals of your family of origin.
3. List your family rules and decide:
    a. Which you still use?
    b. Which have you changed?
    c. Which still give you a problem?
4. What values and beliefs did your family promote?
5. What myths and secrets did (does) your family of origin have or still have?
6. What patterns did you notice within your three generational family system?
7. What would you like to add about your family?
8. What would you like to update or change about your family?
9. What would you like to add to your life?

FAMILY RULES

Instructions: Share your family of origin rules before the age of eighteen. Were there any rules regarding caregiving? If so, what were some of these rules?

COMMUNICATION STANCES

Directions: Select the communication stance(s) that you used most often as a survival message when interacting with the care recipient.

Superreasonable   Irrelevant   Leveling   Placating   Blaming

Share your feelings and experiences with the investigator about the chosen communication stance(s).

THE WHEEL OF INFLUENCE

The wheel of influence is a graphic representation of people who strongly affected your life from birth to present age.

Instructions:

1. Place your name in the circle in the center of the page.
2. Surround your name with smaller circles (as many as necessary).
3. Inside the circles, place the names of those persons you feel significantly *supported, nurtured, guided, directed* or *influenced* you in some way (either positively or negatively). Include relatives, friends, teachers, ministers, etc.
4. Select three adjectives and a role for each person and place it near each circle.
5. Thicken the lines between you and any person who was especially significant in your life and lightly shade the circle of anyone now deceased.
6. Label each adjective as positive or negative.

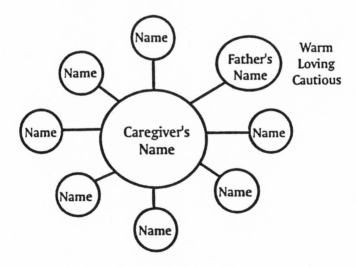

The researcher used the Satir personal iceberg tool as a transformation process technique in which the PFCs shared a typical day of caregiving. The PFCs were given the personal iceberg diagram and asked to start with the "I am" section and proceed upward. The researcher and the PFCs worked with the personal iceberg in a one-to-one context to bring the PFCs "into more self-integration and congruence" (Satir, 1991, p. 173). The researcher interpreted the personal iceberg information to the PFCs.

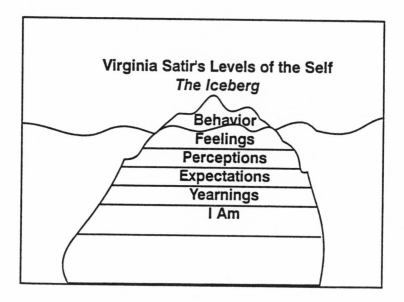

The researcher used the self-mandala as a tool to continue to integrate the PFC's image of the self.

Procedure: Rank order the Mandala (1-8) from the most important to the least important.

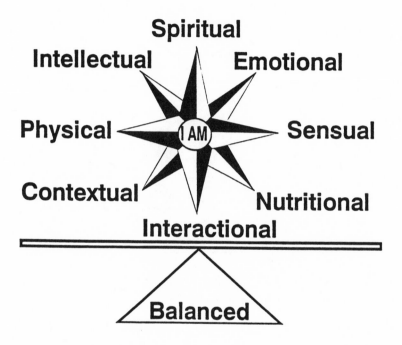

The Mandala is the universal human resources. The "I AM"--basic components of the body.

The Satir self-maintenance kit was used as a teaching tool for the PFCs in a lecturette format. The purpose was to use it as a "symbolic metaphor to increase people's (the PFCs') sense of inner responsibility and self-esteem. The idea is to take greater responsibility and be connected to our deeper source of wisdom" (Satir, 1991, p. 298).

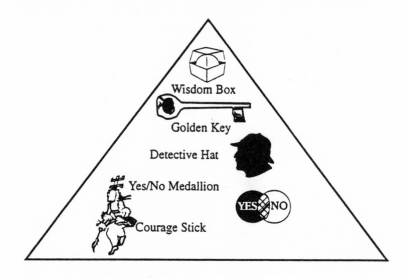

Wisdom Box: Hold the knowledge of your inner resources. These treasures help you move into awareness.

Golden Key: Opens the door to the sanctuary within yourself. Rejoice in the person you are.

Detective Hat: Gives you the ability to figure out life's puzzles with the clues you are given.

Yes/No Medallion: "Yes" on one side, "No" on the other enables you to accept what fits and discard what does not.

Courage Stick: Empowers you to ask for what you want and make your wishes come true.

The Satir change process tool was used to gather data on intergenerational caregiving, rebuilding self-esteem, decreasing enmeshment, burden, and burnout, and increasing health service utilization of the PFC. The researcher used change as an ongoing unconscious process for the nursing intervention. The PFC was given the opportunity, in a one-to-one context of caregiving, to have a cathartic experience of letting go of past feelings. This feedback process provided the researcher with field notes for analyzing each PFC's level of self-esteem, enmeshment, burden, burnout, and rate of health service utilization.

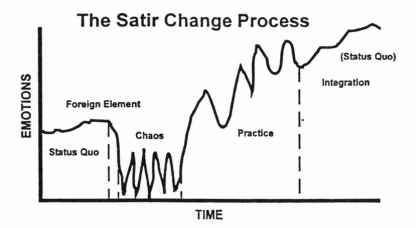

Satir Family Tools used with permission from The Avanta Satir Network, copyrighted ©1996, P.O. Box 66958, Burien, Washington 98166.

Bibliography

Abrahman, P.Y., and Berry, M.L. "Needs of the family caregivers of frail elderly." *Canadian Journal of Public Health*, 83(2) (1992): 147-149.

Alley, J.M. "Family caregiving: Family strains, coping response patterns and caregiver burden." Ph.D. dissertation, Virginia: Virginia Polytechnical Institute and State University, 1988.

Aneshensel, C.S., Pearlin, L.I., Mullan, J.T., Zarit, S.H., and Whitlatch, C.J. *Profiles in caregiving: The unexpected career.* New York: Academic Press, 1995.

Ansell, E.M. "Professional burn-out: Recognition and management." *Journal of the Nurse Anesthetists*, 49 (1981): 135-142.

Archbold, P.G., Stewart, B.J., Greenlick, M.R., and Harvath, T. "Mutuality and preparedness as predictors of caregiver role." *Research in Nursing and Health*, 13(6) (1990): 375-384.

Archer, C.K., and MacLean, M.J. "Husbands and sons as caregivers of chronically ill elderly women." *Journal of Gerontological Social Work*, 21(1-2) (1993): 5-23.

Babins, L., Killion, J., and Merovitz, S. "The effects of validation therapy on disoriented elderly." *Activities, Adaptation and Aging*, 12 (1988): 73-86.

Baillie, V., Norbeck, J., and Barnes, L. "Stress, social support, and psychological distress of family caregivers of the elderly." *Nursing Research*, 37(4) (1988): 217-222.

Banmen, J. "Virginia Satir's family therapy model." *Individual Psychology: The Journal of Adlerian Theory, Research and Practice*, 42(4) (1986): 480-491.

Banmen, J. Conversation with author. 14 July 1991.

Beekman, N. *Family Caregiving, ERIC Digest*, 31 January 1991 (ED 328826).

Bennett, C.E. *The Black population in the United States: March 1994 and 1993*. U.S. Bureau of the Census, Current Population Reports, (pp. 20-480). Washington, D.C., U.S. Government Printing Office, 1995.

Biegel, D.E., Sales, E., and Schulz, R. *Family caregiving in chronic illness: Alzheimer's disease, cancer, heart disease, mental illness and stroke (Vol. I)*. Newbury Park, CA: Family Caregivers Application Series, 1991.

Bienefeld, D., ed. *Verwoerdt's Clinical Geropsychiatry*. Baltimore: Williams and Wilkins, 1990.

Billingsley, A. "Black families and white social sciences." *Journal of Social Issues,* 26 (1990): 127-142.

Blieszner, R., and Alley, J.M. "Family caregiving for the elderly: An overview of resources. *Family Relations*, 39(1) (1990): 97-102.

Bowers, J.E. "Factors influencing family caregiver burden and health." *Western Journal of Nursing Research*, 12(6) (1990): 771-772.

Boykin, A., and Winland-Browny J. "The dark side of caring and challenges of caregiving. *Journal of Gerontological Nursing*, 21(5) (1995): 13-18.

Brody, E. "Filial care of the elderly and changing roles of women (and men)." *Journal of Geriatric Psychiatry*, 19(2) (1986): 175-201.

Bull, M.J. "Factors influencing family caregiver burden and health." *Western Journal of Nursing Research*, 12(6) (1990): 758-770.

Cafferata, G.L., and Stone, R. "The caregiving role: Dimensions of burden and benefits." *Comprehensive Gerontology*, (1989): 57-64.

Cantor, M.H. "Neighbors and friends: An overlooked resource in the informal support system." *Research on Aging*, 4 (1979): 434-463.

Chatters, L.M., Taylor, R.J., and Jackson, J.S. "Size and composition of the informal helper networks of elderly blacks." *Journal of Gerontology*, 40(5) (1985): 605-614.

Chatters, L.M., Taylor, R.J., & Jackson, J.S. "Aged blacks' choices for an informal helpers network." *Journal of Gerontology*, 41(1) (1986): 94-100.

Chenoweth, B., and Spencer, B. "Dementia: The experience of family caregivers." *The Gerontologist*, 26(3) (1986): 267-272.

Clark, M., and Standard, P.L. "Caregiver burden and the structural family model." *Family Community Health*, 18(4) 58-66.

Cohen, D., and Eisdorfer, C. "Depression in family members caring for a relative with Alzheimer's disease." *Journal of American Geriatric Society*, 36(10) (1988): 885-889.

Crossman, L., London, C., and Barry, C. "Older women caring for disabled spouses: A model for supportive services." *The Gerontologist*, 21(5) (1981): 464-470.

Dellasega, C. "Caregiving stress among community caregivers for the elderly: Does institutionalization make a difference?" *Journal of Community Health Nursing*, 8(4) (1991): 197-205.

Dodson, L.S. *Virginia Satir Process of Change*. Binghamton, NY: The Haworth Press, Inc., 1991.

Davidson, J. K. "Respite care of perceptions of burden among family caregivers of frail elderly living at home." Ph.D. dissertation, Peabody College for Teachers of Vanderbilt University, (1989).

Fitterer, K. Conversation with author, 11 April 1994.

Francell, C.G., Conn, V.S., and Gray, D.P. "Families' perceptions of burden of care for chronic mentally ill relatives." *Hospital and Community Psychiatry*, 39(12) (1988): 1296-1300.

Fredman, L., Doly, M.P., and Lazus, A.M. "Burden among white and black caregivers to elderly adults." *Journal of Gerontology*, 50B (1995): 110-118.

Gallagher-Thompson, D., and Steffen, A. "Comparative effectiveness of cognitive/behavioral and brief psychodynamic psychotherapies for the treatment of depression in family caregivers." *Journal of Consulting and Clinical Psychology*, 62 (1994): 543-549.

George, L.K., and Gwyther, L.P. "Caregiver well being: A multidimensional examination of family caregivers of demented adults." *The Gerontologist*, 26(3) (1986): 253-259.

Gerstel, N. and Gallagher, S.K. "Kinkeeping and distress: Gender, recipients of care, and work-family conflict." *Journal of Marriage and the Family*, 55(3) (1993): 598-607.

Gibson, R.C. "Minority aging research: Opportunity and challenge." *Journal of Gerontology*, 44(1) (1989): 52-53.

Givens, B. "Family caregiving for the elderly: Annual review. *Nursing Research*, 9 (1991): 77-101.

Goldstein, V.F. "Coping With Long-Term Illness at Home." Ph.D. dissertation, University of Wisconsin, 1979.

Gonzales, E. Gitlin, L.N., and Lyons, K.J. "Review of the literature African American caregivers of individual with dementia." *Journal of Cultural Diversity*, 2(2) (1995): 40-48.

Harrison, R.M., and Cole, G. " Family dynamics and caregiver burden." *Clinical Geriatric Medicine*, 7(4) (1991): 817-829.

Hernandez, G.G. "Not so benign neglect: Researchers ignore ethnicity in defining family caregiver burden and recommending services." *The Gerontologist*, 31 (1991): 271-272.

Heyman, A., Fillenbaum, G., Prosnitz, B., Raiford, K., Burchett, B., and Clark, C. "Estimated prevalence of dementia among elderly black and white community residents." *Archives of Neurology*, 48 (1991): 594-598.

Hines-Martin, V.P. "A research review: Family caregivers of chronically ill African-American elderly." *Journal of Gerontological Nursing*, 18(2) (1992): 25-29.

Hinrichsen, G.A., and Ramirez, M. "Black and white caregivers: A comparison of their adaptation, adjustment, and service utilization." *The Gerontologist*, 32 (1992): 379-381.

Hogan, S. "Care for the caregiver: Social policies to ease their burden". *Journal of Gerontological Nursing*, 16(5) (1990): 12-17, 40-41.

Hooyman, N.R., & Lustbader, W. *Taking Care: Supporting Older People and Their Families*. New York: The Free Press, 1986.

Horne, J. *Caregiving: Helping An Aging Loved One*. Washington, D.C.: American Association of Retired Persons, 1995.

Jackson, D.G., and Cleary, B.L. "Health promotion strategies for spousal caregivers of chronically ill elders." *Nurse Practitioner Forum*, 6(1) (1995): 10-18.

Jackson, J.J. "Kinship relations among urban blacks." *Journal of Social Behavioral Sciences*, 16 (1970): 1-13.

Jacobson, S.F. "Burnout: A hazard to nursing." In S.F. Jacobson and H.M. McGrath (eds.), *Nurses Under Stress*. New York: John Wiley and Sons, 1983: 98-106.

Jaynes, D.J., & Williams, R.M. *A Common Destiny: Blacks in American Society*. Washington, D.C.: National Academy Press, 1983.

Jed, J. "Social support for caretakers and psychiatric hospitalization." *Hospital and Community Psychiatry*, 40(12) (1989): 1297-1299.

Jones, C.J. "Household activities performed by caregiving women: Results of a daily study." *Journal of Gerontological Social Work*, 23(1/2) (1995): 109-134.

Johnson, C.L., and Barner, B.M. Families and networks among older inner-city blacks. *The Gerontologist*, 30 (1990): 726-733.

Kahn, R.L., Goldfarb, A.I., Pollack, M., and Peck, A. "Brief objective measures for the determination of mental status in the aged." *American Journal of Psychiatry*, 117(4) (1960): 326-328.

Kahana, E., Biegel, D.E., and Wykle, M. (eds.). Family caregiving across the lifespan. *Family Caregiver Applications, Series 4*. Newbury Park, CA: Sage Publications, 1994.

Kane, R., and Kane, R. *Assessing the Elderly*. Lexington: Lexington Books, 1981.

Kart, C.S. "Variation in long-term care service use by aged blacks: Data from the Supplement on Aging. *Journal of Aging and Health*, 3(4) (1991): 511-526.

Kinney, M. *A Handbook for Home-Based Services*. (New York: Educational Resources Information Center, 1979.

Krach, P., and Brooks, J.A. "Identifying the responsibilities and needs of working adults who are primary caregivers." *Journal of Gerontological Nursing*, 21(10) (1995): 41-50.

Kramer, B.J., and Vitaliano, P.P. "Coping: A review of the theoretical frameworks and the measure among caregivers of individuals with dementia." *Journal of Gerontological Social Work*, 23(1) (1995): 151-174.

Krause, N. "Stress, religiosity, and psychological well-being among older blacks." *Journal of Aging and Health*, 4(3) (1992): 412-439.

Lawton, M.P., Brody, E.M., and Saperstein, A.R. *Respite for Caregivers of Alzheimer's Patients: Research and Practice.* New York: Springer, 1991.

Lawton, M.P. "The functional assessment of elderly people." *Journal of the American Geriatric Society*, 19 (1971): 465-480.

Levin, M., Sinclair, I., and Gorbach, P. *Families, Services and Confusion in Old Age.* Brookfield: Avenbury, 1989.

Liebenman, M., and Snowden, L. "Problems in assessing prevalence and membership characteristics of self-help group participants." *Journal of Applied Behavioral Sciences*, 29(2) (1993): 166-180.

Lin, M.N., and Chiou, C.J. "The quality of family care for the elderly homebound stroke victim." *Nursing Research*, 3(2) (1995): 138-148.

Lindgren, C.L. "Burnout and social support in family caregivers." *Western Journal of Nursing Research*, 12(4) (1990): 469-482.

Lowenthal, M.F., and Berkman, P. *Aging and Mental Disorders in San Francisco.* San Francisco, CA: Jossey-Bass, 1967.

Maddox, G. *The Encyclopedia of Aging*, (2nd Ed.) New York: Springer Publishing Company, 1995.

Maslach, C., and Jackson, S. *Maslach Burnout Inventory*, (2nd Ed.). Palo Alto: Consulting Psychologists Press, 1986.

Maslach, C., and Jackson, S. *Maslach Burnout Inventory Manual: Research Edition.* Palo Alto: Consulting Psychologist Press, 1981.

McConnell, S. and Riggs, J.A. "A public policy agenda: Supporting family caregiving," in *Family Caregiving: Agenda for the Future*, M.H. Cantor (Ed.). San Francisco: American Society on Aging, (1994): 25-34.

McElroy, A.M. "Burnout: A review of the literature with application to cancer nursing." *Cancer Nursing*, 5 (1982): 211-217.

McFall, S.H., and Miller, B. "The effect of caregiver burden on nursing home admission of frail older persons." *Journal of Gerontology: Social Sciences*, 47 (1992): S73-79.

McTavish, D.G., and Pirro, E.B. "Contextual content analysis." *Quality & Quantity*, 24 (1990): 245-265.

Mier, S.T. "Toward of a theory of burnout." *Human Relations*, 36(10) (1983): 899-910.

Miller, D., Gulle, N., and McCue, F. "The realities of respite for families, clients, and sponsors." *The Gerontologist*, 26(5) (1986): 467-470.

Mindel, C., Wright, R., and Starrett, R. "Informal and formal health and social support systems of the black and white elderly: A comparative cost approach." *The Gerontologist*, 26 (1986): 279-285.

Montgomery, R., Gonyea, J., and Hooyman, N. "Caregiving and the experience of subjective and objective burden." *Family Relations*, 34 (1985): 19-26.

Moritz, D.J., Kasl, S.V., and Ostfeld, A.M. "The health impact of living with a cognitively impaired elderly spouse." *Journal of Aging and Health*, 4 (1992): 244-267.

Morris, L.W., Morris, R.G., and Britton, P.G. "The relationship between marital intimacy, perceived strain and depression in spouse caregivers of dementia sufferers." *British Journal of Medical Psychology*, 61(9) (1988): 231-236.

Morycz, R.K., Malloy, J., Bozich, M., and Martz, P. "Racial differences in family burden: Clinical implications for social work." *Journal of Gerontological Social Work With Families*, 10(12) (1987): 133-154.

Morycz, R.K. "Caregiving strain and the desire to institutionalize family members with Alzheimer's disease." *Research on Aging*, 7(3) (1985): 329-361.

Motenko, A. "The frustrations, gratifications, and well-being of demential caregivers." *The Gerontologist*, 29(2) (1989): 166-172.

Muhlenkamp, A.J., and Sayles, J.A. "Self-esteem, social support and positive health practices." *Nursing Research*, 35(6) (1986): 334-338.

Mui, A.C. "Caregiving strain among black and white daughter caregivers: A role theory perspective." *The Gerontologist*, 32 (1992): 203-212.

Mutran, E. "Intergenerational family support among blacks and whites: Response to culture or to socio-economic differences." *Journal of Gerontology*, 40 (1985): 382-389.

Neary, M.A. "Community services in the 1990s: Are they meeting the needs of caregivers?" *Journal of Community Health Nursing*, 10(2) (1993): 105-111.

Nolan, M., and Grant, G. "Respite care: Challenging tradition." *British Journal of Nursing*, 1(3) (1992): 129-131.

Norris, J., and Kunes-Connell, M. "Self-esteem disturbance." *Nursing Clinics of North America*, 20(4) (1985): 745-761.

Norusis, M.J. *Statistical Program for the Social Science*. Chicago: SPSS, Inc., 1990.

Newgarten, B.L., Havighurst, R.J., and Tobin, S.S. "The measure of life satisfaction." *Journal of Educational Psychology*, 16(1) (1991) 134-143.

Ogus, E.D. "Burnout and social support systems among ward nurses." *Issues in Mental Health Nursing*, 11 (1990): 267-281.

Olson, D. " Use of FACES II versus FACES III." *Family Inventory Project*. St. Paul: University of Minnesota, 1990.

Olson, D.H., Russel, C.S. and Sprenkle, D.H. *Circumflex Model: Systematic Assessment and Treatment of Families*. New York: Haworth Press, 1989.

Olson, D.H., Bell, R., and Portner, J. *FACES II*. St. Paul: University of Minnesota, 1981.

Olson, D.H., and Killorin, E. *Clinical Rating Scale for the Circumflex Model of Marital and Family Systems*. St. Paul: University of Minnesota, Department of Family Social Science, 1985.

O'Neill, C., and Sorenson, E.S. "Home care of the elderly." *Advance Nursing Science*, 13(4) (1989): 28-37.

Patrick, P.K. "Burnout: Job hazard for health workers." *Hospitals*, 53 (1979): 87-90.

Petchers, M.K., and Milligan, S.E. "Access to health care in a black urban elderly population." *The Gerontologist*, 28(2) (1988): 213-217.

Picot, S.J. "Rewards, cost, and coping of African-American caregiving." *Nursing Research*, 44(3) (1995): 147-152.

Pilisik, M., and Parks, S.H. "Caregiving: When families need help." *Social Work*, 33(5) 1988: 436-440.

Pinkston, E., and Kinsk, N. "Behavioral family intervention with impaired elderly." *The Gerontologist*, 24(6) (1984): 576-583.

Pohl, J.M., Boyd, C., Liang, J., and Given, C.W. "Analysis of the impact of mother-daughter relationships on the commitment to care giving." *Nursing Research*, 44(2) (1995): 68-75.

Poulshock, S., and Deimling, G. "The impact of dementia on the family." *Journal of the American Medical Association*, 248(3) (1984): 333-335.

Pruchno, R.A., and Potashnik, S.L. "Caregiving spouses: Physical and mental health in perspective." *Journal of American Geriatric Society*, 37(8) (1989): 697-705.

Quayhagen, M., and Quayhagen, M. "Differential effects of family-based strategies on Alzheimer's disease." *The Gerontologist*, 29(2) (1989): 150-155.

Rew, L., Bechtel, D., and Sapp A. "Self as an instrument in qualitative research." *Nursing Research*, 42(5) (1993): 300-301.

Robinson, K. "A social skills training program for adult caregivers." *Advances in Nursing Science*, 10(2) (1988): 59-72.

Rosenberg, M. *Society and the Adolescent Self-Esteem*. Princeton, NJ: Princeton University Press, 1965.

Rosenberg, M. *Conceiving the Self.* New York: Basic Books, 1979.

Roybal, E.R. *Exploding the Myths: Caregiving in America*. Washington, D.C.: U.S. Government Printing Office. Committee Publication Number 99-611, 1987.

Roybal, E.F. *The Status of the Black Elderly in the United States*. Washington, D.C.: U.S. Government Printing Office. Committee Publication Number 100-622, 1987.

Rudin, D.J. "Caregiver attitudes regarding utilization and usefulness of respite service for people with Alzheimer's disease." *Journal of Gerontological Social Work*, 23(1/2) (1995): 85-107.

Satir, V., *Conjoint Family Therapy*. Palo Alto, CA: Science and Behavioral Books, Inc., 1961.

Satir, V., *The New Peoplemaking*. Palo Alto, CA: Science and Behavioral Books, Inc., 1988.

Satir, V. and Baldwin, M. *Satir: Step by Step*. Palo Alto, CA: Science and Behavioral Books, Inc., 1983.

Satir, V., and Banmen, J. *Virginia Satir Verbatim 1983*. North Delta, B.C.: Delta Psychological Associates, Inc., 1983.

Satir, V., & Banmen, J., Gerber, J., & Gomori, M. *The Satir Model: Family Therapy and Beyond*. Palo Alto, CA: Science and Behavioral Books, Inc., 1991.

Schaie, K.W., and Lawton, M.F. "Interventions and services for family caregivers." *Annual Review of Gerontology and Geriatrics, II*. New York: Springer Publishing Company, 1991.

Schopler, J., and Galinsky, M. "Support groups as open systems: A model for practice and research." *Health and Social Work*, 18(3) (1993): 195-207.

Schulz, R., and O'Brien, A.T. "Alzheimer's disease caregiving: An overview." *Seminars in Speech and Language*, 15 (1994): 185-194.

Seltzer, M.M., Litchfield, L.C., Kapust, L.R., and Mayer, J.B. "Professional and family collaboration in case management: A hospital-based replication of a community-based study." *Social Work in Health Care*, 17(1) (1992): 1-22.

Shanas, E. "The family as a social support in old age." *The Gerontologist*, 19 (1979): 169-174.

Sheehan, H., Wilson, R., and Marella, L. "The role of the church as providing services for the aging." *Journal of Applied Gerontology*, 7 (1988): 231-241.

Sime, A.M. "Burnout and social support in family caregivers." *Western Journal of Nursing Research*, 12(4) (1990): 484-485.

Skaff, M.M., and Pearlin, L.I. "Caregiving: Role engulfment and the loss of self." *The Gerontologist*, 32(5) (1992): 656-664.

Smerglia, V.L., Deimling, G.T., and Barresi, C.M. "Black/white family comparisons in helping and decision-making networks of impaired elderly." *Family Relations*, 37(3) (1988): 305-309.

Stanwyck, D.J. "Self-esteem through the life span." *Family and Community Health*, August (1983): 11-28.

Stove, R., Cafferata, G.L., and Sange, J. "Caregivers of the frail elderly: A national profile." *The Gerontologist*, 27(5) (1987): 616-626.

Taft, L.B. "Self-esteem in later life: A nursing perspective." *Advances in Nursing Science*, 8(1) (1985): 77-84.

Taylor, R.J. "The extend family as a source of support to elderly blacks." *The Gerontological Society of America*, 25(5), (1985): 488-495.

Taylor, R., and Chatters, L. "Extend family networks of older black adults." *Journal of Gerontology*, 46 (1991): S210-S217.

Taylor, R.J., and Chatters, L.M. "Church-based informal support among aging blacks." *The Gerontologist*, 26 (1986): 637-642.

Thomas, B.L. "Self-esteem and life satisfaction." *Journal of Gerontological Nursing*, 14(2) (1988): 25-30.

Thomas, V., and Olson, D. "Problem families and the circumflex model: Observational assessment using the clinical rating scale (CRS)." *Journal of Marital and Family Therapy*, 19(2) (1993): 159-175.

Townsend, A. "Nursing home care and family caregivers stress." *Stress and Coping in Later Life Families*. J.H. Crowther, S.E. Hobfoll, and D.L. Tennesenbaum (Eds.). Washington, DC: Hemisphere, (1990): 267-285.

U.S. Congress Select Committee on Aging, House of Representatives. *The Chairman's Report on the Black Elderly in America*. Washington, DC: U.S. Government Printing Office (1988): 100-672.

U.S. Congress Select Committee on Aging, House of Representatives. *Improving the Quality of Life for the Black Elderly: Challenges and Opportunities*. Washington, DC: U.S. Government Printing Office, (1988): 100-672.

Vitaliano, P.P., Young, H.M., and Russo, J. "Burden: A review of measures used among caregivers of individuals with dementia." *The Gerontologist*, 31(1) (1991): 67-75.

Wallace, G.W. "Caregiving of homebound elderly: The determinants of burden and the buffering effects of social support on the family caregiver." Ph.D. dissertation, University of Virginia, 1987.

Walls, C.T. "The role of church and family support in the lives of older African-Americans." *Family and Aging*, Summer (1992): 33-36.

Woods, B. "Proximity and hierarchy: Orthogonal dimensions of family interconnectiveness." *Family Process*, 24(4) (1985): 487-507.

Wykle, M. *Family Caregiving, Long-Term Care for Older Adults: A Report of the NINR Priority Expert Panel on Long Term Care.* Bethesda, MD: U.S. Department of Health and Human Services, 1994: 153-173.

Wykle, M., and Segal, M. "A comparison of black and white family caregivers' experience with dementia." *Journal of the National Black Nurses' Association*, 5(1) (1991): 29-46.

Wylie, R.C. *Measures of Self-Concept*. Lincoln, NE: University of Nebraska Press, 1989.

Zarit, S. Conversation with author, 12 April 1994.

Zarit, S., Reever, K., and Bach-Peterson, J. "Relatives of the impaired elderly: Correlates of feelings of burden." *The Gerontologist*, 20(6) (1980): 649-655.

Zarit, S., Orr, N., and Zarit, J. *The Hidden Victims of Alzheimer's Disease: A Family Under Stress*. New York: New York University Press, 1985.

Zarit, S.H., Todd, P.A., and Zarit, J.M. "Subjective burden of husbands and wives as caregivers: A longitudinal study." *The Gerontologist*, 26 (1986): 260-266.

Zarit, S.H., and Whitlatch, C.J. "Institutional placement: Phases of the transition." *The Gerontologist*, 32 (1992): 665-672.

Index

Caregiver Burden, 7, 15, 80
Caregiver Burnout, 7, 16, 81
Case Study, 32
Chronically Ill Frail
Elderly, 6, 29
Control Group, 47, 100-102,
107, 109

Data Collection and Analysis,
48
Definitions, 6

Enmeshment, 6, 7, 14, 27,
74-77
Experiential Teaching-
Learning Cycle, 18, 100,
105
Experimental Group, 30,
100-101, 105, 107, 109

Health Services Utilization,
8, 16, 29, 77
Human Subjects Approval, 48
Hypotheses, 5
Results, 98

Intervention Protocol, 30

Kahn Mental Status
Questionnaire, 59, 100
Katz Activities of Daily
Living, 60, 100

Literature Review, 11

Maslach Caregiver Burnout
Scale, 28, 81, 100
Models, 11-12, 14
Conceptual, 24
Satir, 8, 18, 20
Self-Directed Skills, 6,
11-12, 18, 21, 24, 30,
62, 84, 95, 100-104,
107, 108

Nursing Research, 105-106

Olson Clinical Rating Scale,
27, 107
Olson Enmeshment
(FACES II), 27, 74,
100, 107

Pilot Study, 26
Primary Family Caregiver,
3, 23, 62

Research Findings, 101
Implications, 103
Limitations, 106
Practice, 104
Recommendations, 107
Theory and Education,
105
Rosenberg Self-Esteem Scale,
26, 69, 100

Satir, 18
  Model, 8, 18, 20
  Tools, 6, 8-9, 11, 20, 101
Self-Esteem, 7, 13, 69, 71-73,
  84, 87
Study Instruments, 26

Theoretical Framework, 18

Zarit Caregiver Burden Scale,
  28, 100